Too Wonderful for me

By Bruce Green

© 2025 Spiritbuilding Publishers.
All rights reserved. No part of this book may be reproduced in any form without the written permission of the publisher.

Published by
Spiritbuilding Publishers
9700 Ferry Road, Waynesville, Ohio 45068

TOO WONDERFUL FOR ME
By Bruce Green

All Scripture quotations, unless otherwise indicated, are taken from the Holy Bible, New International Version.
Copyright 1973, 1978, 1984 International Bible Society.
Used by permission of Zondervan Publishing House. *All rights reserved.*

ISBN: 978-1-964-80524-5

Cover Photo by Mackenzie Green

Spiritbuilding
PUBLISHERS

spiritbuilding.com

Table of Contents

Dedication 1
Foreword 2
Introduction 3

An Introduction to Wonder

Tuning in to Wonder 6
Opening Our Eyes to Wonder 9
Has "Wonderful" Lost Its Sense of Wonder? 11
Amazed and Alive to Wonder 13
The Dark Side of Wonder 16

Old Testament

Tents and Altars 20
Starry, Starry Night 22
On a Hill Far Away (1) 24
On a Hill Far Away (2) 26
On a Hill Far Away (3) 28
Seeing the Glory of God (1) 30
Seeing the Glory of God (2) 33
Losing Ourselves in the Glory of God 36
Miriam's Timbrel 38
Dealing with the Detested (Manna, Snakes and Jesus) 40
That's the Story! 43
Surprised by God 46
Reverence and Rejoicing 48

Centering Ourselves 51
The Wonder of His Word 53
Inflating or Inspiring? 57
Under the Broom Tree 60
Growing a Greater Vision of God 63
Isaiah Unraveled 66
Leaving the Consequences to God 68
Less Than Paradise 70

The Gospels

It Seemed Good to Me 74
Ah, Joseph and Mary! 76
Down at the River with John 78
Water into Wine 80
How Much More 82
When a Little Water Gets in Your Boat 84
The Mathematics of Grace 86
An Exalted View 88
Seven Miles from Jerusalem 90

Acts and the Letters

Everywhere They Looked 94
Shaking Things Up 96
Embracing Your Interruptions 98
Gloriously More 100
Glory and the Ordinary 102
God's POV 104
Waking Up Sleepy Saints 107

Subversive Joy 109
The Gratitude of Holiness (1) 112
The Gratitude of Holiness (2) 114
Living as Part Two People 116
Changing the World 118
Living with Longing 120

Examples Today

How Deep the Father's Love for Us 124
I've Never Seen That Before 126
The Music of Heaven 128
Food on Our Plate and Music in the Metro 130
A Great Place to Be 133
A Little Debbie Christmas 135

Afterword 137
Selected Bibliography 141

Dedication

To Chris Tidwell and Kati Williamson.
For their steady stream of encouragement to me
and countless others over the years.

Special Thanks to . . .

Janice Green and *Chris Tidwell* for their generosity of time in reading
this manuscript and offering their invaluable insights.

And, to *Laura Green* for her work as my unfailing
creative consultant and sounding board.

Foreword

When Moses took his sandals off before God, did the desert sand burn his feet? Was there smoke from the bush, and if so, did it fill his nostrils or cause his eyes to tear? Was the wind blowing that day? If it were important for us to know any of these things, we would have been told. What is important was Moses had an encounter with the living God—the creator and sustainer of everything that is, the One who identified Himself as "I AM WHO I AM."

This book is an invitation to take off our sandals and open our hearts and minds to the wonder, majesty, and mystery of God Almighty. For Moses, it would have started with the songs his mother sang and the stories she planted in his heart in his earliest years. It picked up almost eighty years later with a bush that burned but wasn't consumed. It continued with plagues, the Red Sea parting, manna raining down from heaven, the spectacle at Mt. Sinai, and God revealing His glory to him. These things stretched his spirit, drew him closer to Yahweh, and enabled him to fulfill God's purposes. We shouldn't expect anything less from our contemplation of His goodness and glory.

If you're looking for something nicely unified and neatly packaged in what follows, I'm afraid you'll be disappointed. It seems to me that trying to systematize the wonder of God is a little like Qoheleth's chasing after the wind in Ecclesiastes or Job and his friends coming up with a cohesive explanation for everything he had experienced. It's futile, fruitless, and, above all, an exercise in self-deception. Our Father's glory is a subject that is as expansive as the universe.

You'll find some of these pieces simple and straightforward, while others will prod you to think a little more. My hope for all of them is simply to open a few windows, let some fresh air in, and improve our view. May God bless you richly and deeply as you seek to know Him more fully and walk with Him more closely.

Introduction

In Psalm 139, the psalmist is discussing God's ways—specifically as they relate to Yahweh's intimate knowledge of him. He recognizes that not only is he known by God in a way that no one else is capable of (including himself), but in a way that he is unable to fully grasp. It is a way, he confesses, that is "too wonderful for me" (v. 6). It is unfathomable—the word sailors used to use when water was too deep to be measured.

This phrase is also employed by Job in 42.3, used in Psalm 131.1, and can be found in Proverbs 30.18 (ESV). More to the point, phrases like this, expressing absolute incredulity and wonder at some aspect of God, occur over and over in the biblical witness in texts like Exodus 15.11, Romans 11.33–36, Ephesians 3.20–21, and many, many more (you can get started in Psalms).

Then there are the miracles, wonders, and signs that occur throughout the biblical witness. Thomas Jefferson thought they had no place in Scripture, so he quite literally cut them out of a version of the Gospels he produced. The result was an abbreviated account of a diminished Jesus who was not born of a virgin and did not rise from the dead. While disciples are not guilty of anything so brazen, we all, at times, have allowed the extraordinary to become ordinary. Whatever else they might be, the miracles are jaw-dropping excursions into the nature and character of the Father, Son, and Spirit that speak to a larger world and reality than we are capable of empirically knowing. We should treat them as corridors into the transcendent.

Then, of course, there are the stories of men and women who took whatever they knew of this to heart and sold out to God. It's Abraham and Sarah packing up their belongings and heading off to parts unknown. It's Ruth, the Moabite woman, vowing to live and die wherever her Jewish mother-in-law, Naomi, went. It's the teenage David jettisoning Saul's armor to face the great Goliath with nothing but his trust in Yahweh. We can't overlook the three young men on the plains of Dura who chose to be thrown into a blazing furnace rather than bow down before an idol. And there's the hesitant Esther, spurred on by the words of Mordecai, going before King Xerxes. This is but a small sampling (Hebrews 11 will get you started here).

Finally, there's us. What are we going to do in response to the infinitely awesome God revealed in the Bible? Whatever our answer might be, it can't be "not much." We owe Him, each other, and ourselves more than that.

Fast forward to eternity, where we will see and experience God in a way that we don't and can't in this lifetime in, as C.S. Lewis was fond of saying, "the land of the Trinity." Whatever we think God to be, whatever our imaginations are able to produce in concert with Scripture, He will exceed all those expectations. If that is the case, why don't we act more like it now? How can we be so blasé about God? How can we sing "I Stand in Awe of You" or "How Deep the Father's Love for Us" and, thirty minutes later, act as if He doesn't exist? How is it we can pop Him up on our screen for a few hours a week and then minimize Him the rest of the time?

I'm not the first or the last to ask these questions, and I'm grateful for that because I have many more questions than answers. If none of this has scared you off, I invite you to turn the page and join me as we walk through the holy ground of Scripture to think about how to love, adore, and worship God the Father, God the Son, and God the Spirit.

An Introduction to Wonder

Tuning in to Wonder

The whole earth is filled with awe at Your wonders;
where morning dawns, where evening fades,
You call forth songs of joy. (Psalm 65.8)

So how and where do we find wonder?

The longer I live, the more certain I am that we cannot find it. I'm convinced that if we go shopping for wonder, it will all but kill our chances of encountering it. If we search for it, we'll find plenty of counterfeits, knockoffs, and pretenders in the latest technology, the ever-burgeoning entertainment industry, or the latest thing to go viral. They all do a splendid job of keeping us occupied and anesthetized with their pseudo-wonder, but we won't find the real thing in any of these. I'm slowly learning that you don't find wonder; it finds you.

Having said that, I don't want to leave the impression that there is nothing we can do but passively wait and hope for wonder. The truth is, we can welcome it by preparing ourselves to recognize and receive it, for wonder is all around us. It's in the air we breathe, the people we rub shoulders with, and the work we've been given to do. In short, wherever life is, you will find wonder.

Wonder isn't a lot different than the electromagnetic radio waves that flood our airways and enable us to open garage doors, communicate with satellites in space, set up Wi-Fi networks, and talk on our phones. These waves are everywhere, but if we don't have the ability to tune into them, we'll miss them completely. Children are especially adept at experiencing wonder. It seems to be their default setting. Then, one day, they suddenly stop asking ridiculous questions, they no longer look at things from unique perspectives, they become self-aware, and it's all over—they become just like us. Now, I have never been one to nostalgically lament the fact that children grow up (that is the plan, after all), but is there some way they (and we) could remain child-like while growing out of being childish?

I believe there is. I think this is at least part of what Jesus was referring to when He spoke of having the humility of a child in order to enter the kingdom of heaven (Matthew 18.1ff). Nothing is more repellent to wonder than the know-it-all attitude we often display as adults. We know what we want. We know what we don't want. All that stands in the way of us controlling the universe is the ability to make sure everything turns out according to our plans (good luck with that, by the way).

We ready ourselves for wonder by recognizing there are so many things of which we are unaware. After all, when you stop and think about it, what we actually know is minuscule (at best) compared to all we don't know. We prepare ourselves for wonder by acknowledging this and raising our sail to catch the winds of exploration. We embark on the adventure of discovery rather than fossilizing on the tiny island of *I Know So Much*.

Wonder comes calling, then, as we learn to look at life with different eyes. This ultimately begins as we look at Christ—the epitome of wonder (1 Timothy 3.16). We "contemplate the Lord's glory" (2 Corinthians 3.18), which, if we look closely enough, is everywhere and touches everything (Acts 17.28).

Worship and wonder have a symbiotic relationship. Worship helps us to see wonder, and wonder inspires worship. Churches must never trivialize their calling by trying to compete with the Sunday morning thrill-o-ramas. Instead, leaders are called to promote worship and wonder by challenging people to look at life through spiritual lenses (2 Corinthians 4.18).

> *I keep asking that the God of our Lord Jesus Christ, the glorious Father, may give you the Spirit of wisdom and revelation, so that you may know Him better. I pray that the eyes of your heart may be*

enlightened in order that you may know the hope to which He has called you, the riches of His glorious inheritance in His holy people, and His incomparably great power for us who believe. (Ephesians 1.17–19)

That's wonder!

Opening Our Eyes to Wonder

And Elisha prayed, "Open his eyes, LORD, so that he may see."
(2 Kings 6.17)

Our faith is founded on wonder! The Story isn't The Story without the creation of the cosmos, the flood, Isaac's miraculous birth, God's intervention at Mt. Moriah, or Jacob wrestling with the angel (and that's just the first book of the Bible!). These and other things are not incidental items that we can choose to accept or reject according to their degree of popularity or receptivity by our culture. They are part of the very fabric of our faith.

But that's more than okay with disciples because we understand the wonder of the Biblical witness (which would include but not be limited to the miraculous) is not something that burdens us like too much baggage; it is God's world intersecting with ours. And we are absolutely delighted and joyous to possess a record of *some* of the ways He has done that. The miracles Elisha did in connection with the widow of the prophet and later the Shunammite woman (2 Kings 4), Naaman being cured of his leprosy (2 Kings 5), Jonah's aquatic adventures, God using Peter to bring Dorcas back from the dead (Acts 9), or any of Jesus' miracles—they all fill us with hope that radiates into the darkest corners of our lives.

In the end, it boils down to whether or not we choose to believe in God. If we do, then logically speaking, there's absolutely no reason to be surprised by anything in Scripture regarding His ability and power. And while we are constantly amazed by God's ways, it's also true that we've come to expect such things (in a healthy sense) in the way that we would from someone who is good. As the layers are peeled away and you get to know them better, you're not surprised to find decisions, attitudes, and behaviors that reflect their core goodness.

It is the same way with our Father, who is the epitome of goodness. We're not surprised to find out that the God who loved the world so much that He gave His only Son also knows the number of hairs on our head and takes care of the birds of the air and the flowers of the field. Neither are we surprised that He takes no pleasure in the death of the wicked (Ezekiel 18) or that He throws a party whenever a sinner repents (Luke 15).

While it's true that disciples can't always connect all the dots or explain everything to everyone's satisfaction (including our own), that does not make us any different than those who are skeptics or unbelievers. As humans, we're all subject to limitations. As humans, we all have to choose to put our faith in something or Someone. Disciples have chosen to put their faith in God rather than the latest scientific understanding, anthropological model, or cultural belief system.

Our real challenge is not becoming dull to the wonder in God's word and in the world around us. Elisha prayed that God would open the eyes of his servant to the Lord's unseen army (2 Kings 6.17). It was Alexander MacLaren who succinctly observed, "The manifestation, not the presence, of the angel guards was the miracle."

Read the story and think about that!

> *Be good to your servant while I live,*
> *that I may obey Your word.*
> *Open my eyes that I may see*
> *wonderful things in Your law.*
> (Psalm 119.17–18)

Has "Wonderful" Lost Its Sense of Wonder?

Let them give thanks to the Lord for His unfailing love and His wonderful deeds for mankind. (Psalm 107.8)

I have an article in front of me from Merriam-Webster.com on "How 'Wonderful' Lost Its Sense of Wonder." It discusses semantic bleaching—the process by which a word's meaning can fade over time so that what we end up with in its widespread usage is a greatly reduced version of what the word originally conveyed. Words like love, awesome, literally, genius, and forever are all examples of this. Georg von der Gabelentz, the German linguist often credited with this concept, likened bleaching to a thriving, productive worker who has his hours reduced and then is forced into retirement so that he no longer makes the contribution he once did to the workforce.

Bleaching occurs because language is never a stagnant thing (unless it's "dead" like Latin or Sanskrit). It's continually evolving. In the case of bleaching, massive words like "miraculous" that applied to Jesus stilling a storm are now applied to the great play your son or daughter made at their soccer match. A fine play, no doubt, but they defied no laws of nature in making it. Nonetheless, we're lazy; we employ big words to increase the stature of small things, and before you know it—the big words have lost their big meaning.

That's where we are with *wonderful* and a host of other words that once said something significant about God. Now, a word like *awesome* is used to describe someone's new shoes, a current movie, or a teenager's latest crush. Once this happens ("verbicide," as Lewis called it), it's difficult to use the word effectively in reference to God. It would be like if we started using the word *ocean* for mud puddles or *hurricane* to refer to the weather every time it rained. There would be a definite disconnect when we tried to go back and use them to speak of the Atlantic, the Pacific, or when a weather system was being upgraded from a tropical storm.

All of this is worth bringing up because if God has been diminished in our language, it's likely because He has been diminished in our lives. There is a reason the Israelites were commanded to be careful about how they referred to God. Our words reflect our thoughts. If our hearts are right, we will want to think and speak about God in ways that accurately reflect His glory, majesty, and uniqueness. There's a high possibility this will be challenging, and certainly, it will be renewing. Our bleached-out spirits will be revived as we strive to come to grips with His grandeur. As He gets bigger, we'll get better.

It always works that way.

> *You shall not misuse the name of the Lord your God,*
> *for the Lord will not hold anyone guiltless who misuses His name.*
> (Exodus 20.7)

Amazed and Alive to Wonder

Now to Him who is able to do immeasurably more than all we ask or imagine, according to His power that is at work within us" (Ephesians 3.20).

What are we supposed to do with passages like this one? Texts like this are found throughout Ephesians. There's 5.1, where we're told to be "imitators of God" (ESV). (Did Paul know who he's speaking to—then or now?) And how about later in the chapter when he quotes the Genesis 2 text about a man leaving his father and mother and becoming one with his wife—and then he applies it to Christ and the church and refers to it as a "profound mystery" (v. 32). And we haven't even touched on where he talks about the church bearing witness to "rulers and authorities in the heavenly realms" (3.10) or speaks of the church being "the fullness of Him who fills everything in every way" (1.23).

Again, what do we do with these texts? The question isn't just rhetorical; it's practical. We can (and should) exegete them in an effort to understand them to the best of our ability. But these passages belong in a different category than most of what we find in the biblical witness. They are texts that tell us things that are beyond our ability to understand completely.

And that's the point.

Much of what's found in the Bible is quantifiable information. We can dissect, analyze, and classify it for the profit of ourselves and others. There's something healthy about knowing the context of Habakkuk or the difference between the Sabbath day and the Lord's Day. And we're richly blessed by the people who aid us in these areas.

But there's also a danger. And that is if we mistakenly assume that because some of the biblical witness is quantifiable, all of it is, and we reduce the great transcendent truths of Scripture to factoids. If we're not careful, we reduce the Almighty One into something we can dissect, analyze, and classify. There becomes no question about Him we cannot answer.

The truth is, if we think we know everything about God, we don't know anything about God. While it's true that He has disclosed Himself to us through Jesus (John 1.18), it's also true that when painting a picture of God—we don't have anywhere near enough colors or canvas to fully capture the Almighty One (Job 38–39).

But that's okay.

When we look at the giant Redwood and Sequoia trees, the Aurora Borealis, or some other wonder—are we satisfied to flatten them out to a series of statements regarding their physical properties? Of course not! We view these things with the awe and amazement they call for.

We won't apologize for any of the truths we know (why should we?), but we'll also recognize that not all truths call for a learning response. Some truths (such as the ones mentioned at the beginning of this piece) are accepted more than they are understood. The point of them isn't to be broken down into a series of propositions in an attempt to explain everything; they are simply to be received with wonder and awe. For we're not just disciples (learners); we're child-like disciples who must never lose the ability to marvel at the mystery and majesty of our Father.

I listened to a talk show where the host was singing the praises of a certain celebrity. A woman called into the show to state her agreement, citing the fact that the celebrity had visited her mother's restaurant, and she had relayed to her daughter how nice they were. It may very well be true that the celebrity is a nice person—but I doubt that you could truly determine that based on such a limited interaction. I would expect to hear a more qualified conclusion like, "They made a favorable impression" (or words to that effect) rather than a definitive conclusion that suggested they were an authority on the subject.

We have to be oh-so-careful that we don't approach God as though we are an authority on the subject. We know some super solid things about our Father since He has revealed them to us through Christ (John 1.18 and other texts), but no matter how far down the road we are, there is still so much we don't know and understand. It's healthy to keep that in mind and not close ourselves to the wonder and mystery of God. If you can still be amazed, it means you are very much alive.

The Dark Side of Wonder

Will not the Judge of all the earth do right? (Genesis 18.25)

There's wonder to be found in Acts 2, but it might require some preparation on our part. That's because when we normally think of the word wonder (especially as it relates to God), we tend to focus on things that make our heads spin and our hearts swell. (Like the fact that an adult male has 36 trillion cells, 400 cell types, and 60 kinds of tissue!—Psalm 139.14). Since that's the way the word is usually used in reference to God, thinking of it as something that brings us joy and laughter (see Psalm 126) is as it should be.

But there is another side to wonder.

In the same chapter where the word is used to speak about something marvelous connected to God (Acts 2.11), His actions in confirming Jesus as the Messiah (v. 22), and miracles performed by the apostles (v. 43), there is one other occurrence of wonder. It is used in v. 19 to speak of the terrifying things that would happen in connection with the "great and glorious day of the Lord" (v. 20). Here's the complete passage.

> *I will show wonders in the heavens above*
> *and signs on the earth below,*
> *blood and fire and billows of smoke.*
> *The sun will be turned to darkness*
> *and the moon to blood*
> *before the coming of the great and glorious day of the Lord.*

It's not a comforting passage, nor is it meant to be. It's apocalyptic, and I believe it speaks of the judgment that would come upon the Jewish nation as the consequence of centuries of disobedience and rebellion (see the book of Malachi). The nation that had been called to be a blessing to humanity had become a curse through their wickedness, and their end as a commonwealth was in sight. John the Baptizer had addressed this (Matthew 3.7–12), and so did Jesus (Matthew 23.37–24.44). Everyone who called on the name of the Lord would be saved (Acts 2.21, 38; 22.16), but for those who didn't, there would be judgment. This took place in AD 70 when Titus and the Romans swept in and destroyed the city.

And the word "wonders" is used in association with it.

I suppose the initial response of most of us would be that this doesn't seem wonderful, and we would be right on one level. God certainly sees nothing wonderful about it. We've already noted that He takes no pleasure in the death of the wicked (Ezekiel 18.23). We're also told He wants no one to perish but everyone to come to repentance (2 Peter 3.9). When Jesus approached Jerusalem for the final time, "He wept over it" (Luke 19.41). And on His way to the cross, He told people not to weep for Him but for the city (Luke 23.26–31).

But what is to be done when individuals, cities, and nations become so wicked, corrupt, and destructive that they are an imminent, ongoing threat to everyone around them and to the innocent and righteous within them? What do you do when their impenitence boils over without end? Though they are still loved, the only loving thing to do for the rest of the world is to bring judgment on them. We see this throughout the biblical witness in God's judgment on Sodom and Gomorrah, Nineveh, Edom, Assyria, Babylon, and other nations. He also brought judgment against His covenant people, Israel, on several occasions.

All of this underscores the sinfulness of sin. It forces love to make difficult and painful choices. But love cannot be love and allow evil to go endlessly unchecked—there's nothing compassionate or merciful about that! Love is the doctor who waits patiently in the hope that medicine, other treatments, and the body's healing ability will take care of a terrible, ongoing infection in an arm or leg. But if they have to, they will not hesitate to amputate the limb in order to save the body. They will mourn the loss of the limb, and the suffering amputation brings, but they value and will work for the preservation of life above all else.

The other layer that needs to be added is the recognition that we're not physicians. We don't know when the tipping point between keeping a limb or amputating it occurs. We trust the doctor to make that decision. The same thing is true regarding the judgment of God. It's easy to speculate, second guess, and think we have all the data available to make a decision, but of course, we don't. God sees deeds, motives, hearts, interactions, influences, and outcomes in ways we can't imagine. Yet, in the end, it's not primarily a matter of sheer ability (i.e., His omniscience) we put our confidence in. We know that is true about Him—but it's His heart we trust! We know that the Judge of the earth will do what is right. He who did not spare His Son but freely gave Him up for us will do what is good, right, and true. Always.

In the end, the judgment of God is a mystery that will leave us with as many questions as answers (Isaiah 55.8–9). Nonetheless, we absolutely cannot (and should not try to) understand our Father apart from it.

> *From heaven you pronounced judgment,*
> *and the land feared and was quiet—*
> *when you, God, rose up to judge,*
> *to save all the afflicted of the land.*
> *Surely Your wrath against mankind brings You praise,*
> *and the survivors of Your wrath are restrained.*
> (Psalm 76.8–10)

Old Testament

Tents and Altars

"So he built an altar there to the Lord." (Genesis 12.7)

When Abraham arrived in Canaan "at the great tree of Moreh at Shechem," God appeared to him and told Abraham He would give the land he was traveling through to his descendants (v. 6–7). "So he built an altar there to the Lord" (v. 7). He then pitched his tent between Bethel and Ai and built another altar and "called on the name of the Lord" (v. 8). We have then in v. 6–8 a microcosm of Abraham's early travels in Canaan. It is, as others have noted, a story of tents and altars.

The tents are a symbol of pilgrimage. Although Abraham was called to the land, he lived there as a pilgrim. Hebrews 11.9 says,

By faith he made his home in the promised land like a stranger in a foreign country; he lived in tents, as did Isaac and Jacob, who were heirs with him of the same promise.

Abraham didn't live in the best house in a high-end neighborhood—he dwelled in tents—and so did Isaac and Jacob. He was able to do this because "he was looking forward to the city with foundations, whose architect and builder is God" (v. 10).

What about us? It's easy to get attached to this world, isn't it? If we choose to live by sight as many around us do, then we're imposing substantial limitations upon ourselves. It is only through the eye of faith that we are able to see ourselves as citizens of heaven who are only here for a brief period of time. Psalm 84.5 echoes this truth by telling us, "Blessed are those whose strength is in you, whose hearts are set on pilgrimage." Let's keep our hearts set on the pilgrimage we're making, remembering that it's not a foolish thing to give up what we cannot keep to gain what we cannot lose.

The altars that Abraham built were symbols of his devotion to God. We're not told that God commanded Abraham to build these; it seems he built them because it was in his heart to do so. He built them because he wanted to give thanks to God and worship Him.

There's something powerful about a sacred space. That's what these altars were. They were places Abraham set aside from everything else to honor, praise, and seek God. This is how a pilgrim continues to live as a pilgrim. They meet God in sacred spaces.

What if we treated the place where we assemble more like a sacred space? What if we turned off our phones or didn't even bring them in? (The world will be okay for the couple of hours we're inside.) Can you imagine what that could do to our time together? Instead, we walk in with our mocha mocha-choco-latte-datte in one hand and our technology in the other, and our focus is already diluted. We are distracted disciples missing out on the power of sacred space.

We can learn something from Abraham!

Starry, Starry Night

He took him outside and said, "Look up at the sky and count the stars—if indeed you can count them." Then he said to him, "So shall your offspring be."
(Genesis 15.5)

Northern California is home to the giant sequoia trees. According to information from *The Sequoia National Park* website, the tallest of these tops out somewhere around 300 feet with a base circumference of 40 feet. Their branches can be up to 8 feet in diameter, and their bark is 3 feet thick. They weigh up to 2.7 million pounds, and the oldest ones have been around since the time of Solomon.

Not far from the sequoias are the giant redwood trees. The tallest of these is almost 400 feet with a base circumference of 22 feet. Their branches can be up to 5 feet in diameter, and their bark is 12 inches thick. They weigh up to 1.6 million pounds, and the oldest have been around since the time of Christ.

Anyone with a good pair of binoculars can see the seeds in these trees—or, actually, the cones containing the seeds. (The seeds themselves are quite small). The greater challenge is to "see" the trees in the seeds. Although they grow quickly (as high as 30 feet in ten years and 100 feet in 50 years), if you planted them today, it would take somewhere between 500 and 750 years for them to reach their full height. That's something you'd never live to see, so it would require some faith to visualize it.

God took Abraham outside one starry night and had him gaze up at the sky. He told him his descendants would be as innumerable as the stars. Genesis 15.6 says that *"Abraham believed God."*

Some people believe in God in the way they believe in the Grand Canyon—they acknowledge His existence, but it doesn't really affect their lives in any meaningful way. The text doesn't say Abraham believed *in* God; it says he believed God. He trusted in His power, believed in His purpose, and put his life at God's disposal. And because of that, he saw the trees in the seeds.

That's the kind of thing that can happen when we allow God to change our thinking. Before this, Abraham could only see the seeds in the tree and was convinced his servant would inherit everything (v. 2–3). But he was willing to exchange his view of the future for God's—something the people of Babel weren't willing to do (Genesis 9.1 with 11.3–4).

We often think that the greatest move we can make is to a bigger house, a better part of town, a nicer job, etc. It's not. The greatest move we can make is when we move from what we can see and understand to what God can do.

God saw Abraham's faith and said, *"This is a man I can build a nation around. This is a man I can bless the world through."*

And He did just that.

I wonder what God says about us.

On a Hill Far Away (1)

Then God said, "Take your son, your only son, whom you love—Isaac— and go to the region of Moriah. Sacrifice him there as a burnt offering on a mountain I will show you." (Genesis 22.2)

There are passages of Scripture that are profoundly rich, deep, and endlessly expansive. They seem to tower over other texts and have a life of their own. They challenge, inspire, and speak to us on multiple levels. That's more than a subjective impression; Christ said as much in Matthew 22.34ff. and again in 23.23. I think the Akedah (Hebrew for "binding") belongs in this category. What we read there transcends the Genesis account, foreshadows the cross, and speaks in ultimate terms to who God is and what it means to put our trust in Him.

Who is God? This story tells us some things that are initially quite disturbing. God is Someone who told Abraham his son Isaac must be sacrificed. If that wasn't shattering enough, He also wanted Abraham to be the one to put him to death. And He wanted it done in the region of Moriah—meaning Abraham had three torturous days to think about it while they traveled there.

But there's more. The back story is that Abraham and Sarah had been childless, well past the child-bearing age when God promised them a son. Despite the obvious obstacles, Abraham believed God would do this (15.1–6). True to His word, Isaac was born, and God later promised Abraham his descendants would be named through him (21.12). Now, years later, He commanded that Isaac's life be taken. How could God say Abraham's descendants would be named through Isaac and then tell Abraham to sacrifice him (Hebrews 11.17–18)? What kind of sense did that make?

We expect this kind of talk from humans due to our corruption, conflict, and confusion—but not from God. How was Abraham to understand this? The man who had been declared righteous based on believing that

God would make his descendants as numerous as the stars was asked to believe that God was returning him and Sarah back to their barrenness. The promise and the command, given by the same holy God, were spinning uncontrollably in seemingly irresolvable conflict, and Abraham was placed in the position of having to choose one or the other.

What kind of God would ask this of a father and a friend (2 Chronicles 20.7; James 2.23)? What kind of God would put someone through this—someone who had been faithful to Him?

The answer is a God (and Father) who would do the same thing Himself. It doesn't take much imagination to see how what took place at Moriah prefigured what would happen centuries later on a hill called Golgotha. It would also involve a Father and Son, a sacrifice, a painful question, three days, and God providing.

If we see this in its most narrow sense (as something solely between God and Abraham), we're tempted to interpret it in harsh and cruel terms. If we look at it on a broader scale as God intended, it becomes something between He and Abraham that would be used to give the world a window into who He is.

God trusted Abraham to look at it that way, and that's exactly what he did (Genesis 22.8)! Faith is believing in advance what will only make sense in our rearview mirror.

On a Hill Far Away (2)

Some time later God tested Abraham. (Genesis 22.1)

And who is God? He is someone who tests (22.1). This is in direct conflict with the consumer approach to God that views Him as Someone whose sole purpose in creating the entire universe is to make us happy (as opposed to holy). Consequently, anything that gets in the way of a never-ending stream of success, ease, and self-fulfillment is seen as a burden rather than a blessing. It can't be prayed away fast enough because whatever else might be true, we are absolutely sure God doesn't want that in our lives.

But even if we don't think that way, the fact remains that most of us don't appreciate tests. They are painful, meaningful specifics that get in the way of our comfortable, wandering generalities. *Sure, I love You and would do anything for You. What . . . You want to be Lord of my money? You want to reign over my speech? You want me to love the unlovely? Can I get back to You on this?*

If we are unable to appreciate the test itself, maybe we can at least appreciate the purpose behind it. God's "Now I know" (Genesis 22.12) is in some sense accommodative—for James tells us in his discussion of these events (2.21–24) that years before when God counted Abraham's faith for righteousness (Genesis 15.6), Abraham had it in him then to do what God later asked him to do at Moriah. That's why James writes that Genesis 15.6 was *fulfilled* in Abraham offering Isaac (James 2.23). Though the test didn't come for quite a while, his faith in God was there years before. The teacher often already knows exactly what's inside their students—the purpose of the test is simply to draw it out. In this case, Abraham was tested so that his faith might be brought to the fullest light as an example for all. And like any good teacher, God had confidence in His student.

Who is God? He's Someone who tests because He trusts. He has a long, long record of it. He trusted men and women with ridiculously important tasks. He gave Noah the mission of preserving mankind. He had Moses lead Israel out of Egypt and through the wilderness. He picked Joseph and Mary to be the parents of Jesus. He chose 12 very ordinary men to carry on the work His Son began.

He's put His faith in billions of people throughout the ages. He trusts us with life—with prosperity, adversity, time, wealth, possessions, health, talent, relationships, children, and countless other things. Most of all, He trusts us with His Son. Like all who trust, He knows the stabbing disappointment when His faith is violated and broken, but He continues to trust because that is what fathers do.

In the end, we are humbled and honored by His confidence in us. We are grateful that He sees things we cannot see in ourselves and arranges events to bring our faith to the forefront.

That's who God is!

This third I will put into the fire; I will refine them like silver and test them like gold. They will call on My name and I will answer them; I will say, "They are My people," and they will say, "The Lord is our God."
(Zechariah 13.9)

On a Hill Far Away (3)

"The fire and wood are here," Isaac said, "but where is the lamb for the burnt offering?" Abraham answered, "God himself will provide the lamb for the burnt offering, my son." (Genesis 22.7–8)

Is there a more tender scene in Scripture than when the doe-eyed Isaac asks his father where the lamb is for the burnt offering? If that doesn't pierce your heart, you probably need to check for a pulse. And if we find the account difficult to read, what must it have been like for Abraham? Yet he reassures his son that God will provide.

In his commentary on Genesis in the *Interpretation* series (John Knox Press), Walter Brueggemann points out how the narrative of Abraham and Isaac is structured around three similar sections featuring 1) a summons, 2) a response, and 3) an address. The first section (v. 1–2) has God summoning Abraham, him responding ("Here I am"), and an address where God tells him to take Isaac to Moriah and sacrifice him there. The third section (v. 11–12) has the angel of the Lord calling for Abraham, him again responding ("Here I am"), and the address where the angel tells him not to kill Isaac.

The second section (v. 7–8) has all the elements the first and third have. It contains the summons where Isaac says, "Father," the response of Abraham ("Yes, my son?"), and the address asking where the lamb is. But as Brueggemann points out—there is an additional element that breaks the symmetry of the sections and, by doing so, draws attention to itself and becomes the centerpiece of the story. What is this element? It is Abraham's answer to Isaac's question. "God Himself will provide the lamb for the burnt offering, my son." This is the truth that occupies the heart of the story. Everything before and after points toward it.

Who is God? He is Someone who supplies what His creation needs. The God who tests and trusts is ultimately presented in Genesis 22 as the God who provides.

From the mountain in Moriah to the hill of Golgotha, God provided. From the Garden of Eden to the garden where Jesus was resurrected, God provided. From the dawn of creation until the climax of human history, when Christ returns, God provides. This is the theme that Jesus takes up in Matthew 6.25ff and culminates in His instruction for us to "Seek first His kingdom and His righteousness" (v. 33). As disciples, we trust that God will "Give us today our daily bread" (v. 11). The One who will provide for our sins will also provide for every day of our lives.

Brueggemann says, "In the end, our narrative is perhaps not about Abraham being found faithful. It is about God being found faithful." It's not that Abraham didn't demonstrate great faith on this occasion—both the writer of Hebrews and James point to Moriah as an illustration of such (Hebrews 11.17–19; James 2.21–23). What we learn from his example is significant and important. But in the end, maybe what we learn about God, as Brueggemann suggests, is of even greater importance. And what is it we learn about Him?

We learn that God is worthy of the unblinking faith Abraham put in Him.

> *And to this day it is said, 'On the mountain of the Lord it will be provided.'*
> *(Genesis 22.14)*

Holy Father,

How easy it is for us to read this and yet how all-consuming it was for Abraham to live it. Still, You have recorded this for our instruction. With that in mind, we ask that You allow these truths to find the quiet place in our hearts where they might be planted and nurtured so they would bear fruit to Your glory.

Seeing the Glory of God (1)

"Then Moses said, 'Now show me Your glory.'" (Exodus 33.18)

When he made this request to God, Moses wasn't asking for a fireworks display (Rodeheaver). After all, he had been a witness to and participant in some of the most spectacular miracles in history. No, he wanted something more. His desire, as I understand it, was to see God as He was—no pillar of cloud or fire, no cryptic name, no more appearing in whatever forms Yahweh might have chosen to reveal Himself in His previous manifestations (Exodus 16.10, 24.10–11,16–17; Numbers 12.8). He wanted to see God in His essence.

Moses was not making this request as a religious sightseer—someone who only wanted to check a "Wow!" off his bucket list before moving on to the next wonder. No, his situation bordered on desperation. While he had been on the mountain receiving the Ten Commandments from God, Israel had been down on the plain, violating the very law they had promised to obey (Exodus 24.1–8). Rather than imaging the Almighty One who had delivered them from Egypt and the nations around them, they instead had adopted the ways of those nations by seeking to worship (and manipulate) Yahweh through the golden calf (Exodus 32.5–6).

This is where it gets intriguing. While Moses was still on the mountain, God informed him of what had happened with Israel and how He wanted to destroy the nation and start over with just him, but Moses talked Him out of it (32.9–14). God then countered by promising to send an angel with them on their journey to Canaan. He would not personally accompany Israel because they were "a stiff-necked people, and I might destroy you on the way" (33.2–3). Moses' reply to this was as inspiring as it was insightful. He told God that he had no desire to go to the land if He did not go with them (v. 15–16). He was telling Yahweh that he didn't want His gift (Canaan) unless it included Him!

That's significant because, under certain circumstances, we can easily fall in love with the blessings and gifts of God more than God. (Think of Simon in Acts 8.) One of the things that made Moses a great leader was he knew better. To be in the Promised Land without the One who promised it was something he wanted no part of.

George Matheson was a Scottish preacher, writer, and composer of hymns in the 19th century who lost his eyesight when he was twenty years old. Matheson wrote the following in *Moments on the Mount,* which might be dated grammatically, but its message is timeless.

> Whether Thou comest to me in sunshine or in rain, I would take Thee into my heart joyfully. Thou art Thyself more than the sunshine; Thou art Thyself compensation for the rain; it is Thee and not Thy gifts I crave; knock and I shall open unto Thee.

This kind of passion was behind Moses' desire for Yahweh to fully and completely reveal Himself. God had twice spoken of destroying Israel, said He wasn't going to accompany the nation, and then said He would. It seems likely that Moses wanted God to reveal Himself in an ultimate sense so he would know how to properly gauge all this. Seeing His "glory" meant to see Him as He was. It was to see His utter goodness (compare Exodus 33.19 and 22). So, Yahweh accommodated him.

The next morning, "The Lord came down in a cloud and stood there" with Moses. He spoke His covenant name (Yahweh) to him (34.5). He placed Moses in the cleft of the rock and covered him with His hand while He passed by and then removed it so Moses could see His "back." What a text! And yet the occasion was treated with the utmost reverence and dignity—no one other than Moses was allowed on the mountain. The livestock weren't even to graze in front of it (v. 3). Isn't there something to learn here about becoming too casual with God?

The text goes on to say:

> *And He passed in front of Moses, proclaiming, "The LORD, the LORD, the compassionate and gracious God, slow to anger, abounding in love and faithfulness, maintaining love to thousands, and forgiving wickedness, rebellion and sin. Yet he does not leave the guilty unpunished; he punishes the children and their children for the sin of the parents to the third and fourth generation." (Exodus 34.6–7)*

God's self-revelation was verbal as well as visual. For our purposes, it was the part of His self-disclosure that is available to us today. He has revealed Himself to Moses, Israel, and to us through words. But not just any words. They are special words. Although they were initially used to comfort a harried and anxious shepherd who was feeling the weight of the nation on his shoulders, they are intended for all generations.

When it was all over, Moses bowed his head in worship (v. 8). He had "seen" God. Not only did this help him lead Israel to Canaan, but this description of Yahweh is also repeated throughout the Old Testament to help God's people in whatever situation they might be in (Numbers 14.18; Psalm 86.15, 103.8, 145.8, etc.). Do words really have such power?

God thinks they do.

> *For great is His love toward us, and the faithfulness of the LORD endures forever. Praise the LORD. (Psalm 117.2)*

* Exodus 20.5 gives a fuller account of the truth being expressed in the final clause. It says there, "punishing the children for the sin of the parents to the third and fourth generation *of those who hate me*" (emphasis mine). Those people of succeeding generations who hated God (i.e., participated in sin as their parents did) would receive the same punishment as those before them. God punishes people for their own sins, never for the sins of others (Deuteronomy 24.16; Ezekiel 18.20).

Seeing the Glory of God (2)

The Word became flesh and made his dwelling among us. We have seen his glory, the glory of the one and only Son, who came from the Father, full of grace and truth. (John 1.14)

After Israel had completed construction of the tabernacle under Moses' leadership, "the glory of the Lord" filled it (Exodus 40.34). Once again, the nation was provided with an occasion to witness the infinite awesomeness of God. So majestic was the Lord's glory that Moses was unable to enter the tabernacle (v. 35)! Wherever Israel went, God's glory accompanied them (v. 36–38).

If you poked John's gospel with a stick, glory would leak out. The word is used more times there (and in Romans) than in any other New Testament book (17x's). In 1.14, John tells us that the Word became flesh and "made His dwelling" (tabernacled—*Vincent*) among men. As in Moses' time, it was other-worldly and glorious. John wanted his readers to know without a doubt, "We have seen His glory" (v. 14).

He will say in his first letter that they had heard, seen, and touched "the eternal life, which was with the Father and has appeared to us" (1 John 1.2). John and his group bore witness to the glory of God among men. It wasn't the kind of witness where people *think* the getaway vehicle *might* have been dark blue or *maybe* black, late model, two-door or *possibly* four-door. They hadn't been with Jesus for a few seconds—they had lived with Him for a few years. They were certain of what they had seen, and it was His glory!

It can be a real challenge to see the glory of Jesus today. For starters, the Christ of Scripture is often overshadowed by the Christ of culture. The Christ of culture is totally in sync with 21st century values and sensibilities, and everyone is sure they know exactly what He would say and do. He's appropriated for any and every cause. He's pro-life and pro-choice. He's for opening the borders as well as restricting them. He's far-right, far-left, and in the middle. There's no glory in this version of Jesus—He's simply whatever we want Him to be. The Christ of Scripture is anything but predictable and seems to have purposely had very little to do with first-century social and political causes and everything to do with lost and wayward people.

Then, too, Jesus' followers—well, what can you say about the harm we have brought Him? While it's true that critics of Christianity are far too generous in who they count as followers of His, just the same, people of unquestioned faith in Christ have hurt His cause and tarnished His glory.

Forgive us Father.

Still, it's possible that the biggest obstacle to seeing Christ's glory is neither of these. The greatest stumbling block could well be the truth that our default setting is so often to look inward, outward, or downward—but rarely upwards. We miss out on Jesus' glory not because it's not there but because our eyes are somewhere else. We are so enamored with our own little world of shiny things that we miss the transcendent glory of the Lord.

The good news is that it's there whenever we open the Book and read about how He treated people. Yes, He had a deep and abiding love for all people. No tax collector, Samaritan, or leper was beyond His compassion. But He also treated people with great dignity through His refusal to believe (or allow them to believe) that they *had* to remain where they were. He called them higher—from His gentle, probing with the woman at the well to telling the impulsive Peter he would be a rock.

There's glory in His teachings. Who can read the Sermon on the Mount and not marvel at Jesus' wisdom and insight? Then there are stories He told like The Good Samaritan and The Prodigal Son. These teachings transcend time and culture and speak to all people everywhere because it is our Creator speaking to us (John 1.3). On one occasion, the chief priests and Pharisees sent the temple guards to arrest Jesus. They came back empty-handed. When the authorities questioned them about their failure to apprehend Him, they said, "No one ever spoke the way this Man does!" (John 7.46). If God came in the person of Jesus, isn't that exactly what we would expect? They were giving testimony about the glory of the Lord!

Then there are His miracles. They weren't self-promoting spectacles or stunts but acts of compassion that pointed people in heaven's direction. Whether it was the feeding of the 5,000, the calming of the sea, or the raising of Lazarus from the dead, it's not hard to draw a line from these to the glory of Christ. Yet sadly, so many won't do so because they tell us it all just simply sounds too good to be true.

If you have seen His glory, you know that, like Him, it's too good not to be true.

Beyond all question, the mystery from which true godliness springs is great.

He appeared in the flesh,
was vindicated by the Spirit,
was seen by angels,
was preached among the nations,
was believed on in the world,
was taken up in glory.
(1 Timothy 3.16)

Losing Ourselves in the Glory of God

The Lord is my strength and my defense;
He has become my salvation.
He is my God, and I will praise Him,
my father's God, and I will exalt Him. (Exodus 15.2)

What exactly is it that makes us want to sing? It is certainly a way of expressing our moods—emotions set to music. When we are happy, we sing a cheerful song or perhaps even a silly one. When we are down, we sing the blues. But there's more to it than that, isn't there? There is power in singing. Who hasn't sung a song and felt better for it? Who hasn't sung and felt more courageous, committed, inspired, or appreciative? Casandra Martin has this to say:

> *Words engage the mind, music engages the heart and soul. Songs often work their way around the presence of pressure, pride, and perfectionism that tend to hide us, even from ourselves. Music speaks a common language that delights and satisfies hearts around the world. While the form may change, the substance of music has the power to reach deep inside us and captivate our souls.*

We sing because we are made that way. It is something that is hard-wired into us. God created us to sing.

I'm sure that's why singing is something we take great pleasure in doing. Wherever you find people singing, they will almost always be people enjoying themselves. When we're not singing, we take delight in listening to others sing and will even pay (sometimes quite a bit) to hear our favorite singers perform.

So singing isn't going anywhere. It's here to stay because it is a fundamental part of who we are. That said, singing is used in all sorts of ways. There are songs associated with television commercials, political campaigns, movies, etc. Couples have "their" songs, as do schools and universities.

In Exodus 15 we have the record of Moses and the Israelites singing an anthem of praise to God. Yahweh had split the Red Sea so His people could pass through it and then brought the waters back together to drown Pharaoh and his army when they tried to follow. After countless years of oppression, infanticide, and other abuses, the Israelites were finally free of Egypt! Although it looked like Pharaoh would bring them death in the desert (14.10–12), they were delivered. Their sudden reversal spawned an overflow of joy in their hearts and put a song on their lips.

Their song is full of praise for God and what He has done (v. 1–2, 11, 18). Praise is, quite simply, the act of losing ourselves in the glory of God. It is when the sea of self parts, and we walk out and stand in the presence of the Almighty. The waters behind us come back together and drown all our problems—starting with our ego and going on to our fears, anxieties, failures, heartaches, and whatever else has been plaguing us. There is no finer experience. In fact, heaven comes to earth whenever we lose ourselves in the glory of God.

God's glory is the sun bursting through the clouds. It is so magnificent that you cannot look at it directly. It is so bright it banishes all darkness—even the smallest trace amount. All the darkness of suffering, injustice, and pain—it all becomes as if it never was. Praise brings us to that point. We know that however things might work out on this planet and in our tiny lives, God is going to work it all out for eternity. All wrongs will be righted. All impenitence will be dealt with. There will be nothing but glory.

Until then, we work to spread God's kingdom on earth—with joy in our hearts and a song on our lips!

Miriam's Timbrel

Then Miriam the prophet, Aaron's sister, took a timbrel in her hand, and all the women followed her, with timbrels and dancing. Miriam sang to them. "Sing to the Lord, for He is highly exalted. Both horse and driver He has hurled into the sea." (Exodus 15.20–21)

After God had led Israel through the Red Sea and buried Pharaoh and his army beneath the waves, the people of Israel broke into a celebration for the ages. Miriam took out her timbrel (an ancient tambourine) and led the women in dancing and singing as they expressed their jubilation over the deliverance God had brought the nation. Pharaoh and Egypt were finally in their rear-view mirror—never to haunt them again. What an occasion that must have been!

But did you ever wonder about the timbrel? What was it doing in Miriam's possession in the first place? After all, they had to get out of Egypt in a *hurry*. When Pharaoh said, *"Go"* (Exodus 12.31), the people of Israel didn't give him time to change his mind (again). They didn't make reservations, plan an itinerary, or anything like that. They just got out of Egypt as fast as they could. Exodus 12 tells us they didn't even have time to wait for their bread to rise—they just threw it in kneading troughs and covered it with cloth.

Packing in a hurry is challenging. It's not easy in the moment to anticipate what you might need in the days and weeks to come. For Israel, they knew they weren't coming back to Egypt, so they had to take whatever they thought they might need, but they obviously couldn't take everything.

What kind of person in a packing frenzy decides to take a timbrel with her?

The answer is the kind of person planning to celebrate God's deliverance. The kind of person who doesn't know what the future holds amid all of the chaos and uncertainty around her—but she knows Who holds the future.

Whatever else we do, let's remember to pack our timbrel. We will need it because we have a lot of celebrating to do.

> *The Lord is my strength and my defense;*
> *he has become my salvation.*
> *He is my God, and I will praise him,*
> *my father's God, and I will exalt him.* (Exodus 15.2)

Dealing with the Detested
(Manna, Snakes & Jesus)

*"For My thoughts are not your thoughts,
neither are your ways My ways," declares the Lord.
"As the heavens are higher than the earth, so are My ways higher than your
ways and My thoughts than your thoughts."* (Isaiah 55.8–9)

Israel detested the manna. That's what they told God in Numbers 21.5. You remember they had been given the food in response to their grumbling (Exodus 16). After a while, they became bored with the blessing (Numbers 11) and finally reached the point of detesting it. As with all ungrateful people, they didn't realize their response was an indictment of *them* rather than the manna.

So, God sent them snakes—poisonous ones. They had complained about the bread from heaven, so He gave them something from the wilderness. They took issue with the manna that was to preserve their lives, so they experienced the bite of serpents that took the lives of some and left others in great agony and distress (Ronald Allen). They confessed their sin to Moses and asked him to pray for them, and he did. (I'm continually amazed at the great patience and compassion displayed by Moses. He was challenged at every turn and yet responded with amazing grace. He's an example for leaders everywhere!).

God mercifully answered Moses' prayer—but His answer was unlike anything they could have anticipated. He told Moses to fashion a snake out of bronze and put it up on a pole. Whoever looked at the snake would be healed.

God could have saved Israel in any number of ways. He could have just said the word, and it would have been done. But He didn't do that. He chose to heal them in a highly unique way. That He did so encourages us to explore His choice so we might gain insight into His ways.

For instance, looking at the snake on the pole certainly made Israel confront their sin. It would have been impossible to look at the snake without being reminded of the snakes that had bitten them and why it had happened. Complaining was something that had plagued Israel since they left Egypt. They lapsed into it whenever their circumstances became difficult. Looking at the snake was a painful reminder of what they had brought upon themselves. Sigh . . . we've all known that feeling, haven't we?

We also see God's sense of justice. Complaining is a spiritual toxin so He sent poisonous snakes to punish those who had engaged in it. The punishment fit the crime.

Finally, there's the truth that God saved them through something detestable. Snakes were cursed, unclean, and unloved since the garden. That Yahweh used them to punish Israel doesn't surprise us. That He used one to save Israel does. The point in the text seems to be that whether it was detested manna or a detested snake, God could use it to work the nation's salvation. Israel needed to learn to trust and praise Him rather than grumble and complain.

But it doesn't stop there.

The snake wasn't used merely to *save* Israel; it was used to pre-figure Jesus (John 3.14–15). God used a cursed snake to point people to His Son? He did! In the first century, the cross was a shameful way to die (Galatians 3.13; 1 Corinthians 1.23). It was in the same category as snakes. And God used the detested death of Jesus to provide the basis for the world to be reconciled to Him.

The message from Numbers 21 is God is with us. He is in control. And He is good—right down to knowing exactly how to deal with the detested. As we journey through our wilderness, we will come across things we detest as well. This episode teaches us that we are better off focusing on our Father than complaining. He is more powerful than whatever we detest, and He knows exactly how to use it for glory.

One generation commends Your works to another;
they tell of Your mighty acts.
They speak of the glorious splendor of Your majesty—
and I will mediate on Your wonderful works. (Psalm 145.4–5)

That's the Story!

"But Joshua spared Rahab the prostitute, with her family and all who belonged to her, because she hid the men Joshua had sent as spies to Jericho— and she lives among the Israelites to this day." (Joshua 6.25)

There are lots of lessons to learn from Joshua 6, where God causes the walls of Jericho to fall, and Israel captures the city. Here are some of them.

1. **Walls fall to servants, not lords.** From beginning to end, God specified how He wanted everything to happen. Israel's role was simply to carry out His instructions. They weren't in charge; He was. That is always the formula for victory.

2. **Walls fall by faith, not by force.** Israel didn't have the equipment necessary to break through the thick walls of a fortified city like Jericho. However, they had a large enough army to conduct a siege and starve their way into the city. But that would have taken a long time, and God wanted them to understand He was giving them the victory (6.2). No, they weren't going to take it by force; they would take it by faith—by trusting God and following His commands.

Walls today—walls of sin, weakness, fear, and everything else, still fall through faith. And they fall just like they did at Jericho—one day at a time, one step at a time. That's why, as followers of Jesus, all we need to do is to keep putting one foot in front of the other each day for God. He'll take care of the rest.

3. **Walls fall to those who honor God.** Israel honored God by obeying Him. We honor Him the same way. We're not going to be perfect, but we can be persistent. We're going to stumble and fall at times, but by His grace, we can get right back on our feet and continue moving forward. That honors Him.

That's the story of the walls falling in Joshua 6. It's one of the most well-known, best-loved stories in the Bible. Little children have been marching around the city of Jericho in Bible class and at VBS for as long as . . . well, as long as children have been walking.

But what if this is only *some* of the story? What if there's something underneath the story that we don't see because, like everyone else, we get caught up in the trumpets blowing, the people shouting, and the walls falling? I think this is exactly the case. The story within the story has to do not with the Israelites but with one of the Canaanites—a woman named Rahab.

You remember Rahab. She was a woman who was caught up in sexual sin (prostitution). At great risk to herself, she showed kindness by sheltering the two spies sent to Jericho by Joshua. In return for saving their lives, she and her family were spared when Jericho was attacked (v. 25). So, the battle of Jericho wasn't just about the Israelites taking the city; it was also about the rescue of a Canaanite woman named Rahab.

But it wasn't simply a matter of *quid pro quo* — there's more to her story. We learn in Joshua 2.8–11 that Rahab was a believer in the God of Israel. She had heard about Him drying up the Red Sea so His people could go across and how God had brought Israel victory over the kings who opposed them. She believed the Lord had given them the land of Canaan as well. She knew He was God of heaven and earth.

Now we have a sharper focus—Joshua 6 is about the rescue and *redemption* of a Canaanite woman who would become part of Israel (6.25). While He was bringing judgment upon the Canaanites for their ungodliness (Genesis 15.16; Leviticus 18), He was also bringing salvation to the believing Rahab. In the midst of two-and-a-half million Israelites, God was also concerned about a Canaanite woman named Rahab.

But there's still more to the story.

We later learn from the book of Ruth that Rahab married an Israelite named Salmon. They had a son named Boaz. Boaz married Ruth. Ruth was the great-grandmother of David. Jesus was a descendant of David, which means Jesus was a descendant of Rahab! That's exactly what Matthew tells us at the beginning of his gospel (1.5–6, 16).

So, what is going on in Joshua 6? A lot more than we thought! You could say that one of the reasons Israel conquered Jericho was so the woman who would be part of the line through whom Christ would come could be saved. That means it isn't just Israel's redemption we're reading about—it's our redemption as well.

I think that's the way we are to read Scripture.

Surprised by God

Then she arose with her daughters-in-law to return from the country of Moab, for she had heard in the fields of Moab that the Lord had visited his people and given them food. (Ruth 1.6 ESV)

The story of Ruth must have knocked the socks (or at least the sandals) off its Jewish audience. It's the account of a young Moabite woman who, rather than remain in her land with her people upon the death of her Jewish husband, made the radical decision to accompany her mother-in-law (Naomi) to Israel.

Still, this doesn't do justice to the enormity of Ruth's decision, for Naomi strongly discouraged Ruth from going with her (1.11–14) and successfully dissuaded her other daughter-in-law (Orpah), who had the same idea (v. 14).

But it didn't work with Ruth.

She was not just committed to going with Naomi; she had thought through the consequences of her decision. Naomi's people would be her people. Naomi's God would be her God. Where Naomi was buried, Ruth would be buried. This last statement is perhaps the most incredible because, all things being equal, Naomi would probably die a couple of decades before Ruth. Ruth was promising to remain in a foreign land long after Naomi's death out of her desire to honor her. And she invoked Yahweh's wrath upon her if she failed to follow through on all she had spoken (v. 17).

If you were a Jewish person hearing this story, your mind would undoubtedly be spinning. A Moabite woman said these things? Their nation came into existence due to the incestuous relationship between Lot and his oldest daughter (Genesis 19)! And wasn't it Balak, the king of Moab, who tried to employ Balaam to curse Israel (Numbers 22.11)?

Didn't the Moabites eventually seduce Israel into immoral pagan rituals (Numbers 25)? The most jaundiced Israelite would wonder what Ruth's "true agenda" was in returning with Naomi. The less cynical would simply wonder.

And what brought about Naomi's desire to return? She heard "the Lord had visited His people and given them food" (1.6). Where had she heard this good news? In Moab of all places! The ESV says she heard it in the "fields of Moab" (v. 6). In the fields of Moab they were talking about Israel's God! Who would have thought it?

My guess is that there's a lot of talk about God that goes on "in the fields of Moab" that would surprise most of us. For whatever reason, we often limit God's influence and outreach to people outside His kingdom (overlooking the truth that He loves them just as much as He loves us). Then, I think we also don't give people outside His covenant enough credit for their interest in the Almighty. We tend to see it as a cut-and-dried situation—either they're following Him, or they're not interested. The result is that we end up being surprised by God.

That's when the real challenge comes. We can delight in God's surprises and grow with them, recognizing that our old wineskins need to be discarded. Or we can put our heads back inside our shells, surrounded by what is familiar, comfortable—and stifling.

Mark it down. if you serve the Almighty, He will surprise you. Delight in it and the newness it brings.

Reverence and Rejoicing

"How can the ark of the Lord ever come to me?" (2 Samuel 6.9)

David had become king of Judah and Israel—but this didn't happen all at once. He became king of Judah when Saul died (2 Samuel 2.4), and then king of Israel 7½ years later (5.4–5). This reflected the instability that existed among the tribes of Israel. Ish-Bosheth, Saul's son, had been king of Israel prior to David. Abner, the power behind Ish-Bosheth, defected to Judah and was subsequently murdered. Then Ish-Bosheth was killed, and David became king. The kingdom he ruled over was a shaky coalition of competing interests.

Nobody understood this better than David, yet in the events that followed, his actions were not in alignment with either bringing the nation together nor honoring God—the kinds of things we would expect from him. It's not that he didn't say the right things—in 1 Chronicles 13.2–3 he spoke of bringing the ark of the covenant to Jerusalem and how the nation had been without it during the reign of Saul. Even more to the point, he prefaced his plan with "if it is the will of God" (v. 2).

But it wasn't.

God was not okay with the manner in which David planned to transport the ark or his misplaced emphasis on the matter. David fell into the trap of making the situation more about himself than God. After the failed attempt to bring the ark to Jerusalem (and the loss of a man's life), his lament is revealing, "How can the ark of the Lord ever come to me?" (2 Samuel 6.9).

Was that the kind of question a king should have asked at a time like that?

David's preoccupation with his own agenda (i.e., securing his throne) explains why, despite his earlier words about making sure it was the will of God, he would later confess, "We did not inquire of Him about how to do it in the prescribed way" (1 Chronicles 15.13). (It's revealing that David had instead employed the method the pagan Philistines had used in transporting the ark—1 Samuel 6. Whenever God's people take their cues for following God from the world, trouble is sure to follow).

David had used the situation for his agenda rather than God's. He wanted to bring the ark to Jerusalem to assure the northern tribes would come there to worship and thereby secure his rule—hence his "How can the ark of the Lord ever come to me?" But as with Israel in 1 Samuel 4.3ff, who brought the ark against the Philistines to assure their victory while they lived godlessly (7.3–4, 8.8)—God would not be used! Or, when the Philistines captured that ark and tried to use it to proclaim Dagon's glory (1 Samuel 5)—God would not be used! David had acted more like Saul than David, and God would not allow Himself to be used in such a manner.

After Uzzah's death for his "irreverent act" (2 Samuel 6.7), David cycled through a number of emotions. Initially, he was angry (v. 8), then afraid (v. 9), and finally, he was reflective. Over the next three months, he had time to think about what had happened and why. And as we would expect, he amended his ways. His focus shifted from himself to God. The ark was to be transported not on a cart but with poles by the Levites as God had commanded (1 Chronicles 15.2, 11–15). A sacrifice was offered (2 Samuel 6.13). By these actions, David showed his reverence for God.

This episode is instructive. There are people today who never get past being angry with God. Like David, they don't like the way God goes about being God. Unlike David, they make no attempt to understand why He does what He does. In their incomplete and imperfect knowledge, they cast their vote that God is guilty, and that's sadly as far as they ever get with Him.

Then, there are others who are afraid of God. They only see Him in terms of judgment. Again, they do not attempt to grow past this superficial understanding. As a result, they never experience the peace and joy that God created them for.

Maybe one of the reasons David was a man after God's own heart was because he pursued God. He certainly made his share of mistakes. And as we've seen here, he was angry with God and then afraid of Him. But he didn't stop there! He reminded himself what he already knew—that God desired a relationship with him that resulted in peace, joy, and love—and that reverence (rings and poles) was the launching pad. (If your relationship with God doesn't have rings and poles, like David, you need to rethink it.) But if it does, then like David, you should have joy because reverence leads to rejoicing—every time!

Centering Ourselves

Sing joyfully to the Lord, you righteous;
it is fitting for the upright to praise Him. (Psalm 33.1)

For much of history, man believed Earth to be the center of the universe. Then Copernicus, Galileo, Kepler, and others came along and told us that we weren't. "Fine," we said, "If we can't be the center of the universe, then at least we're the center of our galaxy." (If we can't be the biggest kid in the neighborhood, we'll at least be the biggest kid on the street.)

Then, in the early part of the last century, Harlow Shapley and others began to tell us that we're not the center of the galaxy. In fact, we're not even close—we're about 30,000 light-years from the center!

What's true in the scientific realm is also true in the spiritual realm. We are not the center. The humanists are as wrong now as the scientists and religious scholars were when they taught that we were the center of everything. We're not. We're not the answer, we're not the ultimate, and we're not the highest. We're certainly not transcendent.

Most importantly, without acknowledging God, there's no way for us to move out of our eccentricity.

That's where praise comes in. In the act of praise, we center ourselves by putting our out-of-line lives in line with God. It's only by anchoring our identity in Him that we can possess an accurate understanding of who we are. As the Psalmist said.

Know that the Lord Himself is God.
It is He who has made us and we are His;
We are His people,
The sheep of His pasture.
(Psalm 100.3)

In the act of praise, we see ourselves more clearly than at any other time. Our delusions of self-sufficiency are shattered, and out of that shattering, truth, honesty, and integrity emerge.

As the glove can ultimately be defined only in terms of the hand, our truest identity is realized only through relating to our Father. The act of praise becomes much like the hand filling the glove; we gain definition, intimacy, and power.

> *Enter His gates with thanksgiving*
> *And His courts with praise;*
> *Give thanks to Him*
> *And praise His name.*
> (Psalm 100.4)

The Wonder of His Word

Open my eyes that I may see wonderful things in Your law.
(Psalm 119.18)

This text in Psalms is one of several that encourage us to reflect on the glory of God through the wonder of His word. Earlier, we looked at the Akedah (Genesis 22) and saw something of its depth. I want to return to it in this piece and add two more texts to the discussion. Psalm 22 and Isaiah 53. Like Genesis 22, these texts forecasted Christ's crucifixion. To appreciate their predictive element, we need to take a closer look at each passage.

Psalm 22

The psalm belongs to the classification of psalms referred to as laments, prayers for deliverance, or petition psalms. Psalms belonging to this category represent the largest group and constitute roughly a third of the Psalter. Psalm 22, in many ways, is the most expansive in this category. James Mays says, "When one carefully examines the psalm in the context of other prayers for help, it becomes clear that the intensity and the comprehensiveness are a fact of the psalm's composition" (Psalms, Interpretation, John Knox Press).

Mays also cautions us against attempting to understand this psalm in light of Jesus' cross experience. Instead, we should view His experience in light of the psalm. Mays' point is the psalm spoke to Israel for roughly a thousand years before Christ. Although it finds ultimate expression and fulfillment in His sufferings, it is also true that Jesus appropriated the psalm to Himself as a way of identifying with all who had experienced the forsakenness depicted there. At the cross, He took on not just the sin of the world but its suffering as well (1 Peter 2.19–21).

What makes this psalm so powerful is not simply how thoroughly it documents the external events of Jesus' crucifixion (e.g., "They divide my clothes among them and cast lots for my garment" and other details) but also its vivid description of the inner trauma of oppression. It fully captures the cross experience—even though crucifixion wasn't practiced until centuries after the psalm was written.

As the following chart shows, all four gospel writers borrowed from Psalm 22 in their descriptions of the crucifixion.

Psalm 22	Matthew	Mark	Luke	John
v. 1	27:46	15:34		
v. 7	27:39	15:29		
v. 8	27:43			
v. 15				19:28
v. 18	27:35	15:24	23:34	19:24

It's worth noting that while these five verses from Psalm 22 are specifically incorporated by the writers, the whole psalm applies to Jesus. You can look at verses like v. 14 ("I am poured out like water, and all of my bones are out of joint. My heart has turned to wax; it has melted within me"), v. 16 ("Dogs surround me, a pack of villains encircles me; they pierce my hands and my feet") or v. 17 ("All of my bones are on display, people stare and gloat over me") and see how they all speak to Christ's cross experience.

Isaiah 53

The text in Isaiah is like Psalm 22 in that it speaks to Israel as well as being predictive of Jesus. The chapter is part of a larger section of Isaiah where the prophet is speaking to the righteous remnant of the nation (often referred to as "My servant"—42.1, 49.3,6, and other places). As with Psalm 22, this section fits Jesus as He was part of the righteous remnant of Israel and the epitome of a servant of God. But just as with the psalm, it also speaks predictively of Jesus in Messianic terms, and He is the fulfillment of that.

Luke tells us that Jesus applied Isaiah 53 to Himself (see Luke 22.35–37). Peter applied it to Christ's crucifixion (1 Peter 2.20–25). Phillip did the same thing in Acts 8.26–35. As with Psalm 22, you can read through Isaiah 53, and it speaks presciently of Christ's rejection in the crucifixion.

Some Conclusions

We've briefly considered three passages that spoke predictively about the crucifixion of Jesus. Those familiar with Scripture recognize that the predictive element is part of its fabric—but not in a grandstanding way (like a person climbing up the side of a building). Instead, prediction often occurs within the context of a message that also has an immediate meaning, as we have seen in Psalm 22 and Isaiah 53.

Nonetheless, the predictive element of Scripture is there. It wasn't back written after the events occurred to make it look like it was predictive. In anyone's view, these texts were written a long, long time before Jesus' crucifixion and their antiquity is corroborated by the Septuagint and the Dead Sea Scrolls.

Contrast this with our inability to (accurately) forecast the future. People spend staggering amounts of money on gambling, lotteries, and the like because they think they have an intuition regarding the future. Of course, they don't. Their worthless tickets, empty pockets, and barren bank accounts bear witness to humanity's impotence in this realm. We are simply not able to accurately forecast the future. When you get right down to it, we're not even sure what the weather will be like tomorrow!

What, then, will we do with the predictive element of Scripture? In the end, there are only two choices. We can choose to look at the Scripture as the product of man alone and try to evade or ignore its predictive aspect. Or we can recognize what the writers of the biblical witness tell us—that Scripture is the result of man aided by God (2 Timothy 3.16–17; 2 Peter 1:20–21). Over and over, they tirelessly remind us they are telling us what God said. For the disciple, the predictive element is just one of the many fingerprints of God upon the Scripture. And we are in awe of the One who makes known "the end from the beginning" (Isaiah 46.10).

But there's more. We can go down at least another level. The three passages we've looked at are all from the Old Testament. Yet beyond this commonality, there is quite a bit of diversity about them. Moses wrote the material in Genesis 22, David is, in all probability, the author of Psalm 22, and Isaiah wrote Isaiah 53. It gets more intriguing if we keep going. Moses wrote around 1500 BC, David around 1,000 BC, and Isaiah somewhere around 740 BC. Genesis belongs in the Pentateuch, Psalms in the Wisdom literature, and Isaiah to the Prophets.

How is it that these writers, separated by centuries, circumstances, and genres, all spoke to the same future event? How is it their words interlock in the way they do to produce a unified picture of the crucifixion? What precedent do we have in the annals of history or literature (or anything) that compares with what we find in Scripture?

And the deeper you go into the biblical witness, the richer it gets. We are exposed to countless intersections that occur between books written centuries apart. Hebrews shows how Christ is the fulfillment of the old covenant sacrificial system. Matthew's gospel presents Jesus as the Messiah who is restoring the kingdom of David (a theme taken up by Luke in Acts 1). Israel's deliverance in Exodus foreshadows our deliverance in Christ and is developed by many NT writers. In Revelation, John develops truths from visions recorded over 600 years before in Daniel chapters 2 and 7. And on it goes.

It is all there in glorious wonder for anyone to experience. Anyone, that is, who is willing to mine the treasure.

The law of the Lord is perfect, refreshing the soul.
(Psalm 19.7)

Inflating or Inspiring?

*Cause me to understand the way of Your precepts,
that I may meditate on Your wonderful deeds.* (Psalm 119.27)

No one is sure exactly where the word *hype* comes from. Some think it came about by shortening the word hyperbole. Others believe it has something to do with illicit drug use and the hypodermic needle—getting "hyped up." Then there's the thought that it simply comes from the prefix hyper. I suppose one explanation is as good as another—maybe they were all involved in the formation of the word. What we do know is that by some time in the 1960s, the word was being used for "excessive or misleading publicity" (Online *Etymology Dictionary*).

Living in a consumer culture means that hype is all around us. There is news hype, medical hype, sports hype, celebrity hype, political hype, religious hype—it comes in every shape, size, and color. It's as if everyone speaks in all upper-case letters, with exclamation points after everything, and uses *awesome* in every other sentence. Each person is trying to speak louder than the preceding one, as though the importance of what you have to say is somehow determined by the volume at which you say it.

Most hype is simply some form of self-promotion that sooner or later has to do with buying and selling (this is where hype's consumer culture roots show through). With some refreshing exceptions, commercials are hype. They say whatever they think they need to say to increase sales of whatever they're selling. How often do we hear phrases like, *studies show that, critics are calling it,* and *here's what people are saying*? There's usually next to nothing said about *what kind* of studies they were (i.e., their validity and reliability) or *who* the critics or people are (their credibility).

Hype is vacuous. It is froth and bubbles. It's the item you order after seeing it advertised online or on television, and when you receive it, it neither looks like what you saw nor does what it is supposed to do. Hype creates great expectations and often delivers minimally and sometimes not at all.

What is the opposite of hype? Good question. Humility. Hope. Truth. And ... wonder. If you think about it, hype is the sorry substitute the world often dredges up for wonder. It is a wonder wannabe and poseur. True wonder needs no hype, and true hype has nothing to do with wonder.

We are part of a world that, to a significant degree, has lost sight of wonder. We have been numbed by entertainment that never ends, dumbed by a media that does our thinking for us, and insulated by all the technology around us. If we want a natural wonder, we purchase little machines or software that simulate the sound of surf crashing against a coastline or a storm surging. Or we travel the world looking for wonder in half-empty places because the people who live there have also gone somewhere looking for wonder. Our efforts to find wonder are so often fruitless because it's not about *where you* are but *what you are*. If we are out of touch with Him, who is the embodiment of wonder, then it should come as no surprise that we end up with more wander than wonder.

In pointing people to God, churches should direct them to true wonder and stay away from the hype. But too often, they try to bring people to the God of wonder by employing hype. They wade in with an ALL CAPS, !!!'s, and AWESOME!!! approach. Groups that embrace this style typically make it sound as if God is doing so much through them that He couldn't possibly have time to work anywhere else. And despite what Jesus said in Matthew 6.1–5, 16–18, they have no hesitancy in letting everyone know their good deeds. They market Jesus with performance-oriented worship that majors in trendiness, often at the expense of truth. The result of this is a mixed and confusing message because hype creates consumers while wonder creates worshipers, and the two are definitely not compatible.

Hype doesn't inspire; it merely inflates. Wonder inspires. We aren't the wonder, and we are not responsible for trying to churn it up (no matter what the consumer demand might be). We're to take people to the cross and the empty tomb and invite them to see the wonder there, not be hype factories. Our task is to live as the body of Christ—serving, feeding, clothing, and teaching.

By doing these things, we point people to Him, who is the wonder!

Under the Broom Tree

He came to a broom bush, sat down under it and prayed that he might die. "I have had enough, LORD," he said. "Take my life; I am no better than my ancestors." (1 Kings 19.4)

Jezebel and Ahab had plunged Israel into dark and destructive ways. If we think idolatry is simply about bowing down before an idol, we need to do a deeper dive. Leviticus 18 offers an overview of some of the sexual practices and other darkness that flowed from Canaan's idolatry. I don't think we'd be off the mark to understand much of the same kind of thing to have been taking place in Israel during Elijah's time.

Although Ahab was king, it was Jezebel who was the driving force behind much of the wickedness that characterized his reign. She was the one, according to 1 Kings 18.19, who was supporting 850 prophets of Baal and Asherah (Baal's consort). We're also told twice that she was responsible for having the prophets of the Lord put to death (v. 4,13). Later, when Yahweh showed Himself to be the true God on Mt. Carmel and the prophets of Baal were put to death, it was Jezebel who sent a message to Elijah that he would soon join them (19.1–2).

And it pushed the man of God over the edge.

This seasoned soldier—who had been fed by ravens, brought the widow's son back to life, stopped and started the rain through prayer—"was afraid and ran for his life" (19.3). He probably thought what happened on Mt. Carmel would turn Israel around. He could see the credits rolling and hear the music playing.

But it didn't work out that way.

Elijah wasn't the first (or last) person to underestimate the sinfulness of sin. He headed into the wilderness with weariness written all over him from the events of the last 3 ½ years. From his perspective, his circumstances had overrun his resources. He had convinced himself that he was the only person still following God (18.22, 19.10, 14), and all that was left for him was the gnawing uncertainty of when and where Jezebel's men would catch up to him. He stopped under a broom tree and asked God to take his life. He pointedly told Him, "I have had enough" (19.4).

Elijah was sure his story ended there, but it didn't. The God who rained down fire on Mt. Carmel and brought an end to the false prophets could also nurture and revitalize His plaintive prophet.

It's not insignificant that Elijah was first ministered to physically with cycles of sleep and food during his time under the broom tree. Failure to take care of ourselves in these areas can affect our spiritual perspective. Physically refreshed, the prophet embarked on a 40-day journey to Horeb.

Only 40 days weren't required to make a trip of roughly a couple hundred miles. It seems that the unhurried pace at which Elijah traveled provided time for him to decompress and process all that had happened. This reminds us that meditation and prayer are also important components of our spiritual health, and we neglect them to our impoverishment and non-renewal.

Despite these revitalizing measures, Elijah was still struggling when he arrived at Horeb. He spent the night in a cave on the mountain. There, God asked him, "What are you doing here, Elijah?"

Spiritual renewal is often a search for answers we think we are missing. We're convinced if we can just find them, everything will be okay. But we can short-circuit the process if we don't pause to make sure we're asking the right questions. There's power and perspective in such an approach. Think about how many times Jesus answered a question with a question or asked a question to clarify a situation.

While God spoke to Elijah in the present tense, the prophet could only speak in the past tense.

*"I have been very zealous for the L*ORD *God Almighty. The Israelites have rejected Your covenant, torn down Your altars, and put Your prophets to death with the sword. I am the only one left, and now they are trying to kill me too."* (19.10)

Elijah was stuck in his flawed, inadequate perception of the past and, consequently, of God. God sought to knock him off this position with a powerful wind, an earthquake, and fire. He then spoke in a gentle whisper, again asking, "What are you doing here, Elijah?"

But Elijah didn't hear and gave Him the same answer (v. 14).

God told him to go back and gave him work to do. He then shattered his false perception regarding the number of people still following Him—it was 7,000 times larger than Elijah had thought! And as was the case with Elijah, they had been sustained by God's power. The situation was not as bleak as the prophet had supposed because God's power was much greater than he had imagined.

Stirred by this vision of God, he completed the work given to him and then went to be with the Lord f-o-r-e-v-e-r.

> *As they were walking along and talking together, suddenly a chariot of fire and horses of fire appeared and separated the two of them, and Elijah went up to heaven in a whirlwind.* (2 Kings 2.11)

Growing a Greater Vision of God

In the year that King Uzziah died, I saw the Lord, high and exalted, seated on a throne; and the train of His robe filled the temple. (Isaiah 6.1)

The Tipping Point was Malcolm Gladwell's debut book in 2000 and the first of many bestsellers. It probed the forces behind societal change and proposed to explain how "little things can make a big difference" (the book's subtitle). For example, Gladwell popularized the broken window theory. This theory says that when a window in a building is broken, if it is not repaired in a timely manner, soon there will be more broken windows because the message left by the unrepaired window is that no one is paying attention or cares. However, if the window is repaired, the opposite message is conveyed. Thus, a small thing like a broken window can be a tipping point.

Gladwell went on to apply this to graffiti, toll-jumping on the subway, and other misdemeanors. It wasn't all theoretical either; New York City implemented this principle in the 1990s through a law enforcement strategy known as *CompStat*. The increased attention to misdemeanors and promotion of order was accompanied by a decrease in crime across the board.

Like everything, the broken window theory has its share of critics, and even Gladwell has backed off it to a degree. That's all as it should be because good, healthy debate surrounding the identity of any potential tipping point underscores just how important the concept is. In Gladwell's words, it is "the moment of critical mass, the threshold, the boiling point." It is what is responsible for changing something from good to bad or bad to good.

It's not difficult to see this at the spiritual level. After Cain's sacrifice was rejected by God, the Lord appeared to him and said.

Why are you angry? Why is your face downcast? If you do what is right, will you not be accepted? But if you do not do what is right, sin is crouching at your door; it desires to have you, but you must rule over it." (Genesis 4.6–7) God was telling Cain that how he dealt with his sacrifice being rejected would be a tipping point in his life. Cain didn't heed God's words, tipped in the direction of evil, and the rest is sad history.

It seems to me that growing in our vision of God is also a tipping point—a very important one. If God is nothing more to us than a second-hand, warmed-over religious entity, that's no good. If we have a childish or consumer-oriented understanding of Him, that's also problematic. These views of God won't produce the attitudes and actions He is worthy of. What we need is a mature, robust understanding of the Almighty. Such a vision doesn't come from froth and bubbles. It comes from a deep dive into His self-revelation in Scripture and Christ, accompanied by a long obedience in the same direction.

God revealed Himself to the prophet Isaiah (Isaiah 6). If you read the entire chapter, you will see how it was meant to steel him for the difficult work the Lord had for him to do. In much the same way, John shared a vision of God and Jesus with the seven churches of Asia (Revelation 4–5) that enabled them to triumph (12.11). Exposing ourselves to the greatness of the Father, Son, and Spirit will do the same thing for us.

As we begin to see and experience the glory of God, it becomes difficult not to look at things the way He does, love what He loves, and live as He wants us to. His glory begins to transcend and shape our desires. All of this reminds us how looking inward too much paralyzes while looking upward energizes. As we see Him more clearly and experience the cross more deeply, we change. This is the work of God taking place in our lives—transforming us into His image (2 Corinthians 3.18).

Are we allowing God to grow a greater vision of Himself in our lives?

And we all, who with unveiled faces contemplate the Lord's glory, are being transformed into His image with ever-increasing glory, which comes from the Lord, who is the Spirit. (2 Corinthians 3.18)

Isaiah Unraveled

"Woe to me!" I cried. "I am ruined! For I am a man of unclean lips, and I live among a people of unclean lips, and my eyes have seen the King, the LORD Almighty." (Isaiah 6.5)

Let's stick with Isaiah and think about the holiness of God. The prophet initially felt undone in God's presence, and that's not a terrible thing. If the biblical witness teaches us anything, it is that although God is wholly approachable through Jesus, He is nonetheless holy, and we neglect this truth to our spiritual detriment.

God's holiness is often misunderstood. It is often equated almost exclusively with purity, and God is viewed as a distant, detached, intolerant deity who can't have anything to do with us due to our sinfulness—kind of a Pharisee with superpowers. (You have to ignore a massive amount of Scripture to end up with such a small view of God.) For the tender-hearted, this kind of thinking can be absolutely debilitating. No one needs to tell them that they sin and fall short of the glory of God—they know that! What they need is assurance that despite their self-despised waywardness, there is hope for them.

And there is.

God's holiness is our hope.

God's holiness is His wholeness. He is complete and transcendent in every way. He is what we aren't (fragmented and broken down by sin). He is, as the song says, perfect in power, love, and purity.

Rather than thinking about God's holiness as a single attribute (like kindness or anger), we need to view it as the composite of His character. His love is whole; His justice is perfect, and His grace and mercy are complete. Holiness is the rainbow of God's perfect attributes.

Because God is holy, He will always do what is good, right, and true. In the world's ever-shifting sands of values, morality, and ethics, God is the rock that doesn't move. God doesn't correspond with the truth—He is the truth. God doesn't submit Himself to what is right because it doesn't exist independently of Him; what is right is what corresponds with His character.

But how does all of this give us hope?

It's quite simple. Because God is who He is, when He tells us we can draw near to Him through the sacrifice of His Son, we have absolutely no doubts. We know He's not playing games when He offers us forgiveness and life. We understand it's the real thing when He tells us He loves us. This hard side of God is what we build on. He won't enable us, coddle us, humor us, or insult us with *the soft bigotry of low expectations* (Michael Gerson). He will call us to be what He is—holy.

God's holiness is our hope because this is precisely what we need. What we really need isn't the latest upgrade, the coolest app, the trendiest clothing, another selfie, another trip, or more likes—we need a holy God who can make us whole.

The truth is, if God isn't holy, then we have no hope.

Leaving the Consequences to God

*"They will have no fear of bad news;
their hearts are steadfast, trusting in the Lord."* (Psalm 112.7)

In Daniel 6, the Medo-Persians had taken over after defeating Belshazzar and the Babylonians. Daniel (who had to feel like this was déjà vu all over) once again landed on his feet as Darius appointed him as one of three administrators over Babylon. He did so well in this new position that Darius decided he wanted to turn everything over to him (v. 3). He was "trustworthy and neither corrupt nor negligent" (v. 4).

This didn't sit well with the other administrators and satraps, so they did a background check on Daniel to find something incriminating against him. Crickets. Pinning something on Daniel was like nailing jello to a tree—you just couldn't do it!

What's sad is that rather than changing their mind regarding Daniel and appreciating that he was worthy of the position Darius wanted to give him, his co-workers went from bad to worse. As the writer of Proverbs notes, "A fool finds pleasure in wicked schemes" (10.23). Their strategy shifted, and they decided that because Daniel was righteous, the only way they would be able to get anything on him was if it had "something to do with the law of his God" (Daniel 6.5). In other words, they decided to use Daniel's faith against him. That was, by definition, a wicked scheme—but it was also a backhanded compliment to Daniel and his faith (Matthew 5.10–12).

The administrators and satraps had learned that Daniel was a person of prayer, so they went to the king and talked to him about issuing a decree saying that anyone who prayed to any god or human being other than the king over the next thirty days would be thrown into the lions' den. Darius (who was obviously more flattered than discerning) went along with their request, and the decree was made public. Daniel, from his co-workers' perspective, was toast.

But it didn't work out that way.

Daniel did the same thing he had always done—he went home and prayed by the window, giving thanks to God (v. 10). Make no mistake about it—this is where the victory was won. The victory wasn't when Daniel was later rescued from the lions—that was the victory lap. Praying was crossing the goal line; escaping the lions was the points going up on the scoreboard. But we don't always get to see the points on the scoreboard, do we? That's dealt with in chapter 3 when Daniel's friends told Nebuchadnezzar that whether they were saved from the fire or not, they weren't going to bow down to the image (v. 18). What we need to see is that, like his friends, Daniel was leaving the consequences to God.

When we were in Romania a few summers ago, I taught English to a lady named Aurelia. During one of our sessions, she shared with me that her thirteen-year-old daughter had an inoperable brain tumor. When the girl was younger, she had been diagnosed with leukemia, and the family had to spend a year in Rome while she received treatment there. But now, there were no treatment options and nowhere to go. I fumbled for something to say. Aurelia didn't. She reassured me that her daughter was currently well, enjoying her life, and they were leaving the rest up to God. And she didn't blink an eye! Was she emotionally gutted over the situation? I'm sure she was. But she had placed things in God's hands and was moving forward by faith.

If you want to move your spiritual life to a higher level, just start leaving the consequences to God and you'll be amazed at the power and peace that will flow into your life.

Less Than Paradise

Mordecai had a cousin named Hadassah, whom he had brought up because she had neither father nor mother. (Esther 2.7)

The Book of Esther is a head-turner. It's about a Jewish woman (Esther) who parlays a place in the king's harem into becoming queen of Persia. And, oh yes, her cousin (Mordecai—who acts as a father figure) encourages and helps her to accomplish this. Sounds like the latest from *Netflix* or *Hulu*, doesn't it?

But it's not. It's straight out of the Scripture, which makes it problematic rather than trending from the perspective of many. There's so much that sounds so wrong with the story that they don't know where to begin. They wonder why this story has been preserved, much less included in Scripture.

Fair enough.

The place to start is recognizing that many of our cultural sensibilities are just that—*our* cultural sensibilities. Whenever we want to impose them on people in the past, it almost always leads to trouble. After all, do we really want our descendants two hundred years from now to judge us by whatever the standards of their era might be? Probably not. Whether we care to admit it or not, we are all, to some degree, the product of the time in which we live. (Find your yearbook and look at your senior picture if you don't believe me.) And yes, two centuries from now, people will shake their heads over some of the things we do—just accept it and move on.

We make a huge mistake then when we try to squeeze the story of Esther into our 21st-century worldview. Esther wasn't a Disney princess. She was a Jewish person living under Persian rule in the 5th century BC. While we chafe at the idea of arranged marriages, they didn't bat an eye at it. Living under foreign rule might represent a nightmare to many of us, but it was a reality for most people in Esther's time. Being someone else's servant bristles our brow, but they didn't look at it that way. In short, we must park many of our 21st-century sensibilities when we step into Esther's story.

When Esther is taken to be part of the king's harem, we're horrified but neither Esther nor Mordecai seem to have viewed it that way. While Esther was inside the palace letting her character shine, Mordecai was pacing in front of the place where she was staying to find out any information about how she was doing (2.9–11, 15). After she became Queen, he seemed convinced that God had been at work the entire time (4.14 and his actions throughout the book).

And knowing how it all turned out, it would be difficult to argue against him, wouldn't it?

Maybe that gets us to the real point. we're not pleased with how God (who intimately knew every detail of the situation we can only speculate about) rolled all this out. Couldn't He have done things differently? Why did He allow this godly young woman to become the wife of the tyrant we see in the first chapter? (And yet there is nothing in the biblical record to suggest Esther was ever mistreated in this way—in fact, from everything we're told, Xerxes was highly considerate of her—see 5.3, 7.1–2, 8.1ff, 9.11ff.)

Hmm ...

Maybe there's more to this story for us than simply being aghast at the cultural conditions of Esther's time. After all, the biblical witness *majors* in displaying how God's people, through His power, learned to survive and often thrive in far less than ideal circumstances. Joseph was sold into slavery by his brothers as a teenager. Later, he was falsely accused and imprisoned. He not only survived these injustices; he transcended them to become second in Egypt to Pharaoh and was also reconciled with his brothers. Hannah was unable to have children and was part of a polygamous marriage, but God blessed her with a son who became a priest and prophet. Our book is full of powerful stories of hope like these (Romans 15.4).

If the Scripture teaches us anything, it is that while idealized conditions are wonderful and we should work for them, they are not necessary in order to serve God. It might help us to also keep in mind that it was in paradise that rebellion broke out. I remember studying the Bible online with a Muslim woman who lived in Afghanistan when the Taliban took over. I had another student living in Haiti when their president was assassinated. He told me there was violence in the streets (a pregnant woman was shot), and the economy was in the tank. I imagine they found something quite different in these stories of hope than the critics do.

Well, enough of that. Let's sit down with our ten-dollar cup of coffee, open up our Bibles in the comfort of our climate-controlled dwellings, and rant and rave about how God allowed people in biblical times to live under such crude and cruel conditions.

The Gospels

It Seemed Good to Me

It seemed good to me also, having followed all things closely for some time past, to write an orderly account for you, most excellent Theophilus, that you may have certainty concerning the things you have been taught."
(Luke 1.3–4 ESV)

When Luke was writing the introduction to his gospel, he noted two groups of people:

1) "those who from the beginning were eyewitnesses and ministers of the word" (ESV 1.2), and
2) "many" who were compiling "a narrative of the things that have been accomplished among us" (ESV 1.1).

The first group would be the apostles, and the other would be those disciples who came after them. Luke was part of that group. So, he began his treatise to Theophilus by acknowledging the original communicators of the good news and then the others who followed in their wake (of which he was one). If Luke had a literary agent, he would have been tearing his hair out. The last thing you're supposed to do as a writer is say anything that takes away from the uniqueness of what you're writing. But that's precisely what Luke did. He told Theophilus he did what others before him had done and were doing even as he wrote.

Except he didn't say it *exactly* like that.

His precise words were, "It seemed good to me also, having followed all things closely for some time past, to write an orderly account for you, most excellent Theophilus" (v. 3). "It seemed good to me" is Luke's way of saying, I had to be a part of that group. It didn't matter that others had already done this—he had to do it too.

That isn't difficult to understand, is it? He had a passion for the story ("having followed all things closely for some time past"). He had an idea of how he thought it could be presented ("to write an orderly account for you"). And then there was his relationship with Theophilus.

The name means "lover/friend of God" and was probably given to him when he was baptized. "Most excellent" is used in the book of Acts for Roman officials, so it's possible, perhaps even likely, that Theophilus was a Roman official who had become a disciple of Jesus. Maybe in conversing with Luke, he had expressed a desire to have the story of Jesus in written form to help him sort through the different things he heard. That would explain Luke's words, "that you may have certainty concerning the things you have been taught" (v. 4).

If you follow this thread, it gets more interesting. Luke writes the gospel of Luke for his friend Theophilus. Then, he also writes volume two (the book of Acts) for him (see 1.1–2 there). If you do a word count, Luke wrote more of the New Testament than any other writer—almost 28%. The apostle Paul is second (even if you count Hebrews, which probably was not written by him). Paul writing much of the NT makes sense, though, because most of his letters were addressed to churches all over the Roman Empire. Luke and Acts are written to just one person. The most prolific NT writer was not writing for the masses but for a friend. He was not breaking any new ground—just telling an already familiar, cherished story of "all that Jesus began to do and teach."

God did amazing things with Luke's "It seemed good to me." Maybe we should think about whatever seems good to us and get busy doing it!

Ah, Joseph and Mary!

All this took place to fulfill what the Lord had said through the prophet. "The virgin will conceive and give birth to a son, and they will call Him Immanuel" (which means "God with us"). (Matthew 1.22–23)

The angel told Joseph that his beloved Mary was pregnant not by another man as he had supposed, but by the Holy Spirit of God (Matthew 1.20). Joseph had two things to do: embrace Mary and her pregnancy and keep her a virgin until after the birth of Jesus. The first is explicit in the angel's instructions of v. 20–21, but the second is not. I'm assuming this was spelled out to Joseph in further instructions from the angel that Matthew didn't record because we're later told that "Joseph did what the angel of the Lord had commanded him" (v. 24), and part of that was "he did not consummate their marriage until she gave birth to a son" (v. 25).

I share all that to tell you this—I find all this utterly remarkable. Mary conceived through the Holy Spirit before she and Joseph came together as husband and wife in sexual union—I get that. Joseph's plan to divorce her reinforces the fact that they hadn't been together; I understand that as well. But that God had them marry and then refrain from sexual relations so that the virgin would give birth to a son, well . . . that was a risky strategy on His part, don't you think?

This means that God was placing the fulfillment of the prophecy concerning His Son's entrance into the world (Isaiah 7.14) in the hands of two young, hormonally charged newlyweds and their ability to abstain from sexual relations with each other! We rightly speak about having faith in God, but we don't say enough about God's faith in man! God trusts a bride and a groom to remain abstinent. If you believe what many "authorities" and "experts" tell us today, such a belief for *unmarried* young people is ludicrous and totally out of touch with reality—much less for two people living together as husband and wife. But God didn't think so—and praise Him, neither did Joseph and Mary!

Some day in the future, when the people of God are all together and the great deeds of faith are being rehearsed and celebrated, they'll rightly speak of David slaying the giant, Goliath, and Paul traveling all over the world to share Christ with others. They'll be talk of the anointing of Jesus by a different Mary, of Noah's boat building, Abraham and Sarah heading off to who knows where, and Daniel praying despite the lions. And at some point, someone will say something about the two young newlyweds who for the sake of God postponed a marital privilege so they could partner with their Father in His plans for the saving of the world.

And I suspect all conversation will cease as everyone pauses to ponder this honoring of God in the lives of two young people with such tender hearts and true spirits.

May their tribe increase!

Down at the River with John

They came to John and said to him, "Rabbi, that Man who was with you on the other side of the Jordan—the one you testified about—look, He is baptizing, and everyone is going to Him." (John 3.26)

The U.S. Grant Memorial is in Washington, D.C. To the west is the towering Washington Monument, and behind the Memorial to the east is the United States Capitol. The Grant Memorial is no small thing—it is the largest equestrian statue in the country and fourth largest in the world. Still, due to its very location, it tends to be overlooked and undervalued.

John 3.22–30 is like that. This passage is tucked away between the well-known and loved stories of Jesus' nighttime encounter with Nicodemus and His visit with the woman at the well in Samaria. Consequently, what's recorded in these verses is part of the valley between these two great mountains and doesn't get much attention. But as we'll see, that's in perfect harmony with the powerful lesson taught there.

We're told of a dispute that occurred between John's disciples and "a certain Jew over the matter of ceremonial washing" (v. 25). John has previously mentioned six stone jars at the wedding feast in Cana "used by the Jews for ceremonial washing" (2.6). We know from episodes like the ones recorded in Mark 7.1ff and Luke 11.38ff that the Jewish leaders were enamored with such purification rituals. The baptism that John and Jesus (through His disciples) were engaged in had nothing to do with such rituals. What they practiced was from God (Matthew 21.23-27) and was connected with the coming reign of God through Jesus (Matthew 3.1–6). Jesus' conversation with Nicodemus was all about why, as a leader and teacher of the Jews, Nicodemus hadn't submitted to this baptism in preparation for the kingdom (Luke 7.29–30). Despite these differences, because baptism outwardly appeared similar to the Jewish purification rituals, these kinds of discussions probably occurred quite often.

F. F. Bruce suggests that during this dispute between a Jewish man and John's disciples, the man alluded to what was happening on the other side of the Jordan with Jesus and His disciples— "He is baptizing, and everyone is going to Him" (John 2.26). This is the kind of thing that had previously been said regarding John and his work (Mark 1.5). In musical terms, John's disciples understood they were in danger of going from first chair to second. They were clearly upset at the way Jesus' numbers were tracking. What were they going to do? They would go tell John.

John's response to their concern was like a bucket of cold water thrown in their faces. He pointedly told them three things. First, this was of God (John 3.27). This was in harmony with what he had previously told them (v. 28). (It's noteworthy that John's disciples seemed to have had as much trouble understanding his ultimate purpose as the disciples of Jesus did regarding Christ's mission.) His third point is prefaced by wedding imagery—the best man setting everything up for the bride and groom. When they came together, the best man's job was done, and he was full of joy (v. 29). With this, John was telling them his work was completed and "He must become greater; I must become less" (v. 30).

These words testify to John's greatness. His disciples had jealousy, but he had joy. They wanted him to do something to reclaim his status; he wanted to lose it to Jesus. What kind of person does such a thing?

Someone who understands ~~what~~ Who life is about.

Water into Wine

They have no more wine. (John 2.3)

Numerous contemporaries of Jesus speak of good wine as *not* possessing intoxicating qualities (Pliny, Plutarch, Horace, etc.). In fact, they describe in detail the measures taken to produce such a drink. There's no reason, then, other than cultural bias or biblical ignorance, for insisting that when the master of the banquet spoke of what Jesus made as "choice wine" or "the best" (John 2.10), that it had to be intoxicating. And there are a boatload of reasons for believing it wasn't. (Are we to believe the sinless Christ produced 120 to 180 gallons *more* of intoxicating drink? All of this would be at odds with Proverbs 20.1, 23.29–35, 31.4–6, etc.).

But that's not what I want to talk about. We just needed to get that out of the way so we could move on to the real point of John 2: the power of Jesus to turn water into wine. Moses turned the water into blood, but Christ turned it into something flavorful and delicious.

Water is necessary for life, and we are encouraged by those in the know to drink plenty of it. But it wouldn't be the drink of choice for a wedding. A wedding is a celebration of God's creation purposes. It reminds us of His declaration that *It is not good for man to be alone,* His grace in making a counterpart for Adam, and the intimacy of her being made from the man himself. From one, God made two, so He might join the two back together as one. All of that and more is in play when Christ and His disciples participated in the joyous event at Cana.

As we step inside the story, you can feel the celebratory atmosphere. It was a festive occasion, and everyone was enjoying themselves, as evidenced by the concern when the wine ran out—it had the potential to put a damper on everything. But Jesus stepped in and turned ordinary water into rich, flavorful wine. And yes, He helped a family avoid a social disaster. And yes, He gave a young couple a wedding they would never forget. However, the overarching truth we are to walk away with is that Jesus has the power to turn the ordinary into the exceptional. That's why the miracle manifested His glory (v. 11).

If you think about it, that's really what Jesus has done in our lives—He's turned our water into wine. He's turned our alienation and estrangement into reconciliation, our emptiness into purpose, our fear into faith, and so much more. He's filled our dry, thirsty lives with His Spirit. He has lavished His love upon us. Paul says, "we boast in the hope of the glory of God" and "glory in our sufferings" (Romans 5.2–3). Yes, Jesus has most definitely turned our water into wine.

As disciples, we must be careful not to turn the wine back into water.

As well-intentioned as we might be, it's still nonetheless true that we have the capacity to take the glorious wine that Jesus made and turn it back into tasteless water. It can happen if we define ourselves by what we're against rather than what we're for. It can happen if we focus on the church instead of Jesus. It can happen when we act as if God's commands are burdensome rather than blessings (1 John 5.3). It can happen when we show more enthusiasm about the temporary than the eternal. In short, it can happen when we lose sight of what we have through Jesus.

Let's live like people who have had their water turned into wine by Jesus and be ready when invitations come our way.

How Much More

If you, then, though you are evil, know how to give good gifts to your children, how much more will your Father in heaven give good gifts to those who ask Him! (Jesus in Matthew 7.11)

The size of the observable universe is estimated to be 93 billion light years from one "end" to the other. But that's not the complete story. Our universe also appears to be not only expanding but accelerating—at a rate beyond the speed of light. This isn't supposed to be possible (smile). Adam Reiss, an astrophysicist at Johns Hopkins University and Nobel Prize recipient stated, "It appears there is something missing in our understanding of the universe."

He sounds like a wise man.

I think there is something of this when Paul speaks of how we are known intimately and loved ultimately in Ephesians 3.17–19:

> *I pray that you, being rooted and established in love, may have power, together with all the Lord's holy people, to grasp how wide and long and high and deep is the love of Christ, and to know this love that surpasses knowledge—that you may be filled to the measure of all the fullness of God.*

Got that?

God's love is so much greater than any reference point we have for love. In our efforts to understand divine love, we turn to examples of human love because, well . . . that's the best we can do. There's certainly nothing wrong with this—Jesus did the same thing in Matthew 7.11. He used parental love (flawed and imperfect in comparison to God's holy love) as a launching point for understanding divine love—so we're not off base in doing the same thing. However, the words "how much more" need to be in all caps, bold-faced, italicized, and underlined because they instruct us as to the very real gap that exists between earthly and heavenly love. Human love is extremely helpful in understanding our Father's love, but it has its limitations. Parental love is powerful, deep, and strong. Still, it's a little hard to compare it to God's love for humanity. It's like comparing our solar system to the universe. They are both glorious but on much different scales.

Where does all that leave us? While we can certainly have a strong, basic grasp of God's love, we can and do join the company of those who recognize it is "too wonderful for me." We joyfully accept and embrace our Father's love more than we understand it and express this to Him by the way we think, speak, and act.

There are numerous benefits to making peace with God's transcendent love. The first is that it allows God to be God and us not to be—that's always healthy as humility is a cornerstone of Christian character and life. Then it also tremendously affects how we view forgiveness. If we humanize our Father's love, we will likely do the same thing with His forgiveness and wonder if and how His love can eclipse our sin. We will end up as a question mark rather than an exclamation point and that is helpful to no one. But if we embrace the "how much more" aspect of our Father's love, we won't stumble over how His grace can be greater than our sin (Romans 5.17ff). Finally, all of this should leave us with a deeper, more profound sense of wonder, celebration, worship, and gratitude regarding God.

That's never a bad thing.

God's love for us is the transcendent force in our lives that provides meaning, strength, and hope in all circumstances and situations. To embrace it is to allow the fundamental power behind all creation to drive our lives. To reject it or to under-emphasize it is to wobble down the road of life with punctured tires slapping the pavement.

Does anyone want to ride in that vehicle?

When a Little Water Gets in Your Boat

"They were terrified and asked each other, 'Who is this? Even the wind and the waves obey Him!'" (Mark 4.41)

Mark presents the familiar story of Jesus calming the storm through a series of contrasts (4.35–41). There is an initial contrast in the early actions of the story (Jesus is asleep while the disciples are afraid). Then there is the contrast between their question ("Teacher, don't you care if we drown?") and Jesus' questions ("Why are you so afraid? Do you still have no faith?"). Finally, there is a contrast between the disciples' initial fear of the storm and their fear at the end of this incident ("They were terrified and asked each other, "Who is this? Even the wind and the waves obey Him!").

Let's start with Jesus. It's a miracle to us that He could sleep through such a storm! That's certainly attributable to His trust in His Father, but I think it's also worth thinking about the fatigue He must have experienced at times like this during His ministry. We're in a section where the demands being made on Him were non-stop. The whole purpose of their trip across the lake was to get away from the people for a while. If He had stayed on land, the crowd there would have continued their pursuit of Him.

Regarding the disciples, it should be noted that at least four of them were fishermen, so a little water in the boat wouldn't bother them, but clearly, this was not the case. It was a "furious squall" (v. 37)—the kind of thing they recognized as being beyond their experience and ability.

Nonetheless, they weren't alone—Jesus was with them. And they had seen Him do amazing things. He had healed people, cast out demons, and they had even heard those beings bear witness to His identity as the

Son of God (3.11). But now, with the sea raging, the boat rocking, and Jesus sleeping, they took counsel from their fear rather than their faith. There's no one reading this who can't relate.

They didn't care for the way Jesus was handling the situation and woke Him. They questioned His caring. Jesus spoke first to the wind and the waves like someone would talk to their young child or an over friendly pet. Everything became "completely calm" (v. 39).

Then, He spoke to His disciples. He asked them why they were so afraid. Hadn't He told them they were going to the other side (v. 35)? Didn't they believe He could get them there? This is why He follows with, "Do you still have no faith?" (v. 40). It's worth noting that despite all this, Jesus still got the disciples to the other side of the lake as He said He would (see 1 Thessalonians 5.23–24). This whole scene reminds me of the fundamental truth that we're not saved because we're great—we're saved because God is great! Remembering this will help us on our journey.

The episode ends the only way it can. Rather than being stung by Jesus' sharp words, the disciples were "terrified" by the great miracle they had just witnessed Him perform. Although they had diminished and marginalized Him only moments before, they seemed to realize they had seriously underestimated His ability and identity.

That's a step in the right direction.

If Mark wrote this to disciples in Rome (and there's good reason to believe he did), then the storm clouds that came with Nero's persecution of the church were either on their way or were possibly even the occasion for his writing. Either way, the disciples would need a deeply rooted faith (Mark 4.6, 16–17) if they were to survive the storm. They would need to understand that Jesus was more than capable of getting them to the other side. The fact that Jesus' kingdom is alive and well and Rome's kingdom is long gone is evidence that's exactly what they did. *What do we do when a little water gets in our boat?*

The Mathematics of Grace

I tell you that in the same way there will be more rejoicing in heaven over one sinner who repents than over ninety-nine righteous persons who do not need to repent. (Luke 15.7)

Is there a more difficult scenario for a parent than to be estranged from one of their adult children whose precise whereabouts are unknown? I suppose there could be something, but it's hard to fathom (and who really wants to try?). But suppose you were in this situation (and may God bless and uphold those of you who are). The rest of us can only imagine the gnawing concern that would be ours and how difficult it would be to think of anything else. As our other children comforted us and helped in whatever way they could, we would be pleased by their efforts. Their support would be no small thing, but neither would it diminish our sense of loss.

That's the story we're given in Luke 15.11ff. It is the third and final story Jesus told in response to the complaint of the Pharisees and teachers of the law that "This man welcomes sinners and eats with them" (v. 2). Luke, who features the table prominently in his gospel, has shown Jesus eating with all sorts of people. sinners and tax collectors (5.29ff); Pharisees (7.36ff, 11.37ff, 14.1ff); and close friends (10.38ff). He tells us in 15.1 that "The tax collectors and sinners were all gathering around to hear Jesus." Note they were not eating—they were there to listen to Jesus. This showed that Jesus' approach (being a friend to sinners) was not surprisingly superior to the Pharisee's approach (a failure to even be friendly to sinners). There was nothing left for them to do but "mutter" (v. 2).

But there was something left for Jesus to do, and He shared with them these three stories in an effort to help them see the heart of God that values rescue even more than righteousness. The first story captures this well as the shepherd leaves ninety-nine sheep to go after the one that is missing. Why would someone do that? Because the ninety-nine are "safe" and the lost one is not! This is precisely why there is more joy over the lost sinner who is found than for the ninety-nine who weren't lost.

The mathematics of grace are astounding, aren't they? Does God put any value on ninety-nine righteous people? You know He does! The Scripture is full of texts, from Psalm 1 to the Sermon on the Mount, that teach us this. So, however we understand Jesus here, He's not minimizing righteousness.

What He is doing is maximizing the importance of rescue. This becomes even clearer in the story of the two sons. The father is pleased with the presence and righteousness of the older brother (though, as with all righteous people, he's not without some issues of his own). He withholds nothing from him but tells him, "We had to celebrate and be glad because this brother of yours was dead and is alive again; he was lost and is found" (v. 32). The father's righteousness is mature and complete—he looks at the unrighteous (in this case, his younger son) and longs for his rescue. The righteousness the older brother displays is immature and incomplete because his thoughts were dominated by personal resentment rather than the rescue of his brother.

We would feel the same way the father did if our lost child was found, wouldn't we? If one of our other children pouted about all the fuss and attention given to the rescued child, we would say something similar to what he said. The difference (and it's rather astounding) is that God feels this way about every person on the planet. He is in pain over their lostness and wants nothing more than to rejoice over their rescue.

This speaks volumes to churches, leaders, and disciples about our tendency to become smug and self-satisfied with "business as usual." To have the heart of our Father means there is always an emptiness there as long as anyone is away from God!

An Exalted View

"Thomas said to Him, 'My Lord and my God!'" (John 20.28)

David Blaine is an illusionist and stunt performer who has been in the public eye for many years. In 2020, he attached himself to more than 50 large balloons and floated upward to almost 25,000 feet over the Great Basin Desert in northern Arizona. As he was ascending, he spoke of having the *most unbelievable view in the world ... it doesn't even look like I'm on earth.*

While I suppose you could debate whether he was technically on earth or not, there's no doubt as to what he was looking at when he spoke these words. He was looking at the same landscape he'd studied extensively in his preparation for the event. He was looking at the earth, and he knew that, but we understand the intent of his words—he was seeing everything from a much different perspective—while floating through the air thousands of feet above the ground. Of course, things looked different. He had an exalted view.

I imagine this was something of the way Thomas felt when he saw Jesus after His resurrection. You remember he wasn't there with the other disciples on Sunday evening after Jesus had risen. When they later shared with Thomas what had happened, he didn't believe them. He told them, *Unless I see the nail marks in His hands and put my finger where the nails were, and put my hand into His side, I will not believe* (20.25).

It's not difficult to track Thomas' thinking. The disciples had been on a roller coaster ride with Jesus. They'd seen and experienced things they never dreamed possible. They had gone from fishermen, tax collectors, and other common occupations to being disciples of Jesus—the most extraordinary person who ever lived.

Then it all came crashing down.

Thomas was devastated. From his perspective, the absolute last thing he wanted to do was to engage in some flight of fantasy that suggested Jesus was somehow alive and everything was okay. He had died. He couldn't explain what the other disciples had seen—but it wasn't Jesus—it was a hallucination of some kind. Jesus was dead. Joseph and Nicodemus had taken His body, prepared it for burial, and placed it in a tomb. It was all over and Thomas' world was shattered. If the other disciples wanted to pretend everything was all right that was their business—but he wanted no part of it. He was done with Jesus. Then Jesus appeared to him.

And suddenly, this man who had been around Jesus for the past three-and-a-half years saw Him in a way he'd never seen Him before. He was Lord and God. Well, that's not quite what he said, is it? His actual words were *My Lord and my God*. It was personal for him. That's what happens when you see things from an exalted perspective.

It's easy to look at life with eyes weary from disappointment, pain, heartache—all the things Thomas had experienced—and make the decision not to believe in order to prevent more sorrow and disappointment (Exodus 6.9). And while the specifics of the headlines may change, we still get a large serving of bad news delivered to us every day. However, as Thomas learned, appearance is not necessarily reality. We need to take a deep breath and allow God to open our eyes and give us an exalted view.

> *Then I looked and heard the voice of many angels, numbering thousands upon thousands, and ten thousand times ten thousand. They encircled the throne and the living creatures and the elders. In a loud voice they were saying, "Worthy is the Lamb, who was slain, to receive power and wealth and wisdom and strength and honor and glory and praise!" Then I heard every creature in heaven and on earth and under the earth and on the sea, and all that is in them, saying: "To Him who sits on the throne and to the Lamb be praise and honor and glory and power, forever and ever!" The four living creatures said, "Amen," and the elders fell down and worshiped.* (Revelation 5.11–14)

Seven Miles from Jerusalem

Now that same day two of them were going to a village called Emmaus, about seven miles from Jerusalem. (Luke 24.13)

Two disciples were headed to Emmaus after attending the Passover Feast. But that was not what was on their hearts and minds. They were thinking about Jesus of Nazareth and how He had been turned over to the Romans for crucifixion by the Jewish leaders. To make matters even worse, it was the third day since this occurred, and apparently, something had happened to His body. His tomb had been disturbed, and His body was nowhere to be found. You wonder how many pilgrims who attended the Feast were trudging home entertaining similar thoughts.

They were joined by the resurrected Jesus—only "they were kept from recognizing Him" (v. 16). I suppose it's natural for us to question why this concealing was done. Hadn't these two suffered enough—wouldn't the sensitive thing be to immediately reveal Himself and deliver them from their despondency? While I think you could make a good case for that, Christ regarded it as a teachable moment—one that would not have occurred if He revealed Himself immediately to them. He was taking the longer view of things with them. And by recording it years later, Luke was doing the same for Theophilus and others who would read his gospel.

This longer view interestingly points us away from personally experiencing the resurrected Christ as the apostles and a substantial amount of other people did (1 Corinthians 15.5–8) and toward the witness of Scripture. It was the same thing Jesus told Thomas when He said to him, "Because you have seen Me, you have believed; blessed are those who have not seen and yet have believed" (John 20.29). John then segues from this event to explain that he had written his gospel so that people might believe in Jesus and find life (v. 30–31). While we are to appreciate those who bore witness to the risen Christ, they are very much the exception rather than the rule. That's why a blessing is attached to those who come to faith through the witness of Scripture.

Returning to Jesus and the two disciples, it's important to note that the issue was more than just the resurrection of Christ. They were missing out on something else that was just as fundamental—they were stumbling over the suffering of Christ ("Did not the Messiah have to suffer these things and then enter His glory?"—Luke 24.26). It was this point that Jesus developed as He explained the Scriptures to them (v. 27). It was this point that Peter had stumbled over after his great confession of Christ (Matthew 16.21–23).

It is not insignificant that this limited understanding took them seven miles from where they needed to be (which was in Jerusalem—24.47, 52). They were still close, in the vicinity, within walking distance—just not where they should have been. I can't help but think that there are many today who are seven miles from Jerusalem. They believe in the Christ and wish to follow Him, but they don't want the cross that Jesus brings (Matthew 16.24–25). They embrace the glory, but not the suffering that goes with it (Romans 5.2–5, 8.17–18).

I remember reading about four believers in Nigeria who were killed by Fulani herdsmen a few years ago in the ongoing violence there. The people of the village the men were part of decided to sleep outside so they could get away quickly when they heard the herdsmen or members of Boko Haram coming at night to raid their village. Church leaders discussed "what if" scenarios with disciples (What if you are threatened with death if you don't denounce Christ and similar situations?). Considering this and other persecutions taking place around the world (check out *The Voice of the Martyrs* website), our desire (at times) for God to take away any pain or discomfort the moment it dots our horizon is embarrassing as well as ill-informed. We never consider that it might be a teachable moment or that He might be putting us in such a situation to transform us and/or bear witness to others.

Luke would have us know that Jesus was with two disciples in Emmaus, but when He opened their eyes, they were no longer satisfied to be seven miles from Jerusalem.

Neither should we.

Acts and the Letters

Everywhere They Looked

We hear them declaring the wonders of God in our own tongues. (Acts 2.11)

Wouldn't you love to know *exactly* what the apostles were saying that Pentecost morning when they were "declaring the wonders of God?" Were they speaking of the astonishing reversal of events God had brought about by the resurrection of Jesus? Or was their topic the recently witnessed ascension of Christ? Perhaps they spoke of His epoch-shattering return one day as the angels had promised (Acts 1.10–11).

Whatever it was, it was personalized for those visiting Jerusalem during the feast as they heard about the wonders in their own languages (see v. 6, 8–11). The pilgrims were "utterly amazed" that uneducated Galileans were somehow able to speak in their languages (Acts 2.4, 7). If you're keeping score, there was awe at both *what* the apostles were saying and *how* they were able to communicate it.

Whatever it was they said, it came as a result of the Spirit's enabling (v. 4), and the Spirit led them to speak about the wonders of God. I love that—the Spirit did not lead these men to speak about Himself but God. And like people talking about someone they love, the Spirit spared no praise, no language, and didn't care that some would ridicule what was going on (v. 13). (As amazing as it is, there are always those who will mock the miraculous.)

The wonders of God the apostles spoke of served as a prelude to Peter's message concerning Jesus. It was a message unlike anything ever spoken before. For the first time ever, God's redemptive work in Jesus through the cross and resurrection was presented, and people were told what to do in response to it. I suppose you could think of it as the premiere of the gospel of Jesus. But instead of movie stars, A-listers, paparazzi, red carpets, and limousines, there were thousands of Jewish worshipers, a sprinkling of disciples, the outpouring of the Spirit, and the proclamation about the risen Savior and Lord of transcendent glory. One is hype at its worst; the other is hope at its best.

This was the same gospel that was in God's heart before the foundation of the world (1 Peter 1.20). It was foreshadowed by Abraham and Isaac at Moriah, prefigured in the story of Joseph, and typified by the Passover Lamb and the Red Sea crossing. It had been realized in the events of Jesus' life, death, and resurrection and was then proclaimed to the nations at Jerusalem. All people could be reconciled to their Maker through Him. What had fallen apart at a tree in a garden had been restored through a different kind of tree and in another garden.
Is there anything more wondrous?

And what was the response to this grand unveiling of God's work through Jesus—the One accredited to Israel with "miracles, wonders and signs" (Acts 2.22)? Thousands were "cut to the heart" (v. 37). That's what happens when your eyes are opened to the wonder of God—it hits you deep inside—all the way to your core. But the good news is more than convicting, it is also converting. They were told to turn from their corrupt ways ("repent") and be immersed in the name of Jesus so their sins would be forgiven and they would receive the promised Holy Spirit (v. 33, 38–39). That day, three thousand did just that as they were immersed and embraced God's wonder in Jesus.

Luke goes on to tell us that these disciples "devoted" themselves to their newfound faith (v. 42). They were in an environment of awe due to "the many wonders and signs" that the apostles were performing (v. 43). Gladness radiated and rippled through the community and was witnessed by their sharing with and caring for each other. They experienced favor with everyone, and each day, more people became followers of Christ. And they praised God!

How could they not? There was wonder everywhere they looked. *Many, LORD my God, are the wonders You have done, the things You planned for us. None can compare with You; were I to speak and tell of Your deeds, they would be too many to declare.* (Psalm 40.5)

Shaking Things Up

Now, Lord, consider their threats and enable Your
servants to speak Your word with great boldness.
Stretch out Your hand to heal and to perform signs and wonders
through the name of Your holy servant Jesus. (Acts 4.29–30)

I've often marveled at this prayer spoken by the church in response to the release of Peter and John from their brief imprisonment. To begin with, it's interesting that Luke chose to record this prayer when you would have to assume that there was a great amount of praying done *before* the release of these two apostles (see Acts 12.5ff for an example of such). But what really fascinates (and convicts) me is the content of their petition.

They essentially asked God for two things: that He would take care of His business (consider the threats against the believers, heal, and perform signs and wonders) and that they might be enabled to take care of theirs (speaking with great boldness). Of special interest is that God would "consider their threats." This was placed totally in God's hands. They didn't start a petition drive, get on social media, or hire a lawyer to sue the Sanhedrin—they simply asked Him to note what was said (v. 29). They didn't ask for special protection or that He might prevent anything. What they did ask was that they might speak courageously.

With a prayer like that, it's little wonder that when they were done, the place was shaking, and they were filled with the Spirit. Their request to speak boldly was also granted (v. 31), but that seems to be just the start of things. Sometime later, all the apostles were arrested. This time, some in the Sanhedrin wanted them put to death (5.33). But after some words from a man named Gamaliel, they settled for having them flogged (v. 40). Then Luke records for us the reaction of the apostles to all this—"The apostles left the Sanhedrin, rejoicing because they had been counted worthy of suffering disgrace for the Name," (v. 41). Oh, and one more thing. "Day after day, in the temple courts and from house to house, they never stopped teaching and proclaiming the good news that Jesus is the Messiah," (v. 42).

Their prayer was answered (as all prayers are), but theirs was answered in the sense that they received what they prayed for. God had Luke write it down as an example for all disciples. What will help our churches grow and glorify God? I suppose a lot of things would be helpful, but this should be at the top of the list—bigger prayers make better churches!

Think about that the next time you pray. It might just shake things up.

Embracing Your Interruptions

"Those who had been scattered preached the word wherever they went."
(Acts 8.4)

A young man and woman were in love and wanted to get married. The young man asked her father for his blessing. The man told him, "Before I can give you my blessing, you have to pass the test." The young man wanted to know, "What is the test?" The man replied, "Come to our farm on Saturday morning and you'll find out."

He showed up at the farm on Saturday morning. His fiancée's father told him, "The test is simple. I am going to run three animals at you, one at a time. All you have to do is grab the tail of one of those animals and you'll receive my blessing."

The first animal out of the chute was a cow—only it wasn't the meandering type—it was in full gallop and stopped only to raise back on its hind legs. The young man thought he could possibly grab its tail, but he didn't want to take the chance of getting knocked down and hurt. He looked at the man and said, "Pass."

The man nodded and out of the chute came the second animal—a large dog running straight toward him at full speed. The young man couldn't tell if it was friendly or ferocious and he didn't want to take the chance, so he looked at the man and said, "Pass." He realized he was down to his last chance, but he also knew there wasn't a bull on the farm, and he couldn't think of anything else that might pose a problem. He decided the test was probably about him being smart enough to wait it out and get an easy animal. He was pleased he had waited.

Sure enough, out of the chute hobbled an old cat. The young man looked over at his fiancée's father to let him know he was good with this animal. But when he did, he saw the man was already looking at him with a big grin on his face. The young man was confused until the cat came closer and he realized—it didn't have a tail!

The moral of the story is if you're waiting for the perfect opportunity before you act, you'll be waiting a long, long time. And, while you're waiting, you'll let some important opportunities pass by that you will later regret.

When the church at Jerusalem was scattered because of persecution, Luke tells us, "Those who had been scattered preached the word wherever they went" (Acts 8.4). Rather than see themselves as victims or spend all their time and energy trying to return to Jerusalem, they saw what had happened to them as an opportunity to reach out to the people around them with the good news of Jesus. They didn't wait until everything in their lives was perfect. They had an opportunity outlook.

Our lives move to a different level when we embrace our interruptions and think about how they might be used for God. I doubt if being scattered was on anyone's list of things to do, but those disciples thought about how it could be used for God and kingdom things started happening.

What interruptions do you need to embrace?

Gloriously More

"All things are yours, whether Paul or Apollos or Cephas or the world or life or death or the present or the future—all are yours, and you are of Christ, and Christ is of God. " (1 Corinthians 3.21–23)

When Napoleon Bonaparte and Josephine were engaged in 1796, he gave her a ring composed of two tear-shaped stones—a diamond and a blue sapphire set in opposite directions on a slim gold band. Each stone weighs slightly less than a carat. The ring is relatively modest considering the people involved but reflects the fact that, at the time, Napoleon was a young officer, and that was likely all he could afford.

In 2013, the ring came into the hands of the French auction house Osenat. Interestingly, the auction house asked for the ring to be appraised independently of its provenance. Emily Villane, who oversaw the auction of the ring explained, "It's not our job to tell bidders how much they should pay for the historical premium." Based on the stones, the setting, and the gold band, the ring's value was determined to be about $20,000.

How much did the ring sell for when it was auctioned? Forty-seven times that amount (close to a million dollars)! The people bidding on the ring knew its story and bid accordingly. They understood that the ring's value was so much more than just that of the materials it was composed of—it was part of something much bigger than itself!

The world likes to measure people the same way the appraiser assessed the ring. People are looked at in terms of their physical features, education, occupation, bank account, their followers, their likes, and whatever else is currently considered important. All these parts are thrown on a scale and we're told that's who we are. It's an ugly little business that's made even worse when we accept it and allow it to shape our lives.

But it's not true.

We are much more than the sum of our parts! We belong to something much bigger than ourselves. In the words of the Hebrew writer, we are part of a kingdom that "cannot be shaken" (Hebrews 12.28). That's important because the thing about establishing your identity based on your health, wealth, status, etc., is that all those things, sooner or later, will be shaken. But if you're part of the glorious kingdom of God, not only will you not be shaken—you will realize everything you were created to be.

The disciples at Corinth hadn't grown to the point of seeing this bigger picture. They were confused about their identity, and consequently, they competed against each other. *You follow Peter? Well, I'm better because I follow Apollos!* (chapter 1). *You have the gift of prophecy? Well, I'm better because I speak in tongues!* (chapters 12–14). That's why we find in chapter 13 Paul's words on the centrality of love.

The disciples at Corinth had impoverished themselves by adopting isolationist identities. Paul wanted them to understand they were part of something much bigger than themselves because they belonged to Jesus. He told them, "All things are yours, whether Paul or Apollos or Cephas or the world or life or death or the present or the future—all are yours, and you are of Christ, and Christ is of God (1 Corinthians 3.22–23). Their worldly understanding was blinding them to the glorious realities of Jesus' reign. Their petty views were impoverishing them—all things belonged to them by virtue of their relationship to Jesus.

As disciples, we must not allow the world to push us through its mold (see Romans 12.2) and see only the ring. By God's grace, we need to understand we are part of something gloriously more.

Glory and the Ordinary

For whenever you eat this bread and drink this cup, you proclaim the Lord's death until he comes. (1 Corinthians 11.26)

I don't mean to suggest that there is no wonder in the familiar. Wonder and novelty are certainly not the same and shouldn't be confused. But wonder is harder to spot in the familiar because . . . well, it's familiar. And that leads us to something generally not associated with wonder but is absolutely essential to it—discipline.

Whatever else we might think about discipline, most of us are certain it has absolutely nothing to do with wonder. The word invokes images of hard work, tedious routine, and boring regimentation. While some or all these things are often involved, there is also a paradox to discipline that we must appreciate.

For all of its negative connotations, it's also true that few things of significance are accomplished apart from discipline. No great novel was ever written or a beautiful symphony composed without it. No one, from Einstein to Edison, just "happened" on their amazing discoveries and inventions. Musicians and athletes who perform with such marvelous grace do so only because they have spent untold hours mastering what they do. If discipline is involved in the production of such things, it really shouldn't surprise us that it has an important and vital connection to wonder. Its connection is this: discipline enables us to focus our minds to see the wonder around us that the unfocused pass right by.

Think about how this applies to something like communion. If you look at communion from a minimalist, unfocused perspective, there's little wonder involved—a group of people eating small pieces of unleavened bread and drinking grape juice from tiny cups. Indeed, it looks more strange than wondrous—like an adult version of a child's tea party.

But to the *believer* (and that's the key), so much more is taking place. The disciple understands the bread and juice to be connected with the body and blood of Jesus (Matthew 26.26ff). Through His sacrifice on the cross (and subsequent resurrection), the heavens have opened, and we can have fellowship and intimacy with the Father in a new and ultimate way—unlike anything before (Hebrews 10.19ff). Therefore, observance of the Supper is not only an acknowledgment and celebration of the fact that God is reconciling humanity but a recognition that in the process, He is bringing them together as one in the church, the body of Christ (1 Corinthians 12.13, 27). That being so, there is an incredible richness and depth to this simple ceremony that is inexhaustible. Nonetheless, it takes the tool of discipline to mine the wonder that resides in this memorial. That's why words like *remembrance, examine,* and *discerning* are employed in the Scripture when speaking of our participation in this memorial. They underscore the role discipline plays in focusing our minds to see the wonder that is everywhere in the Supper.

Of course, this approach spills over into all of life. Discipline helps us to see that a sunset is more than an atmospheric phenomenon resulting from our planet's rotation—it is part of the work of God in our daily world. Discipline enables us to understand babies are more than a blending of two people's genetic material—they are "fearfully and wonderfully made" (Psalm 139.14). A rainbow is more than the refraction of light by the sun's rays, it is the promise of our Father (Genesis 9.12ff).

There's glory in the ordinary if we train ourselves to see it!

God's POV

We demolish arguments and every pretension that sets itself up against the knowledge of God, and we take captive every thought to make it obedient to Christ. (2 Corinthians 10.5)

Paul had something to say in 2 Corinthians 10! It was something he had been building toward the entire letter. It concerned a problem that had been brewing at Corinth for quite some time. Things weren't as they should have been because some disciples weren't as they should have been. They complained, they criticized, and they questioned Paul's authority. Paul addressed them in the final section of his letter which begins in chapter 10.

He appealed to them "by the humility and gentleness of Christ" (v. 1). As Scott notes, no one could accuse Paul of "weakness" with this appeal because he links it to the Lord and however they might have looked at Paul—no one thought there was anything weak about Jesus! And what a lovely appeal this is. In a better world, this would lead to the end of whatever needed resolving because, in the name of Christ, we'd all be motivated to work out whatever the problem or issue was. But sadly, in the world we live that's not always the case, and neither was it in Paul's time. Some of the Corinthians had said Paul was bold in his letters but "timid" in person—but Paul told them if things didn't change with some of them, they would find out how wrong they were (v. 2)!

He would wage war—but not in the way the world did because his weaponry was not of this world. That should get our attention. Paul could write, teach, argue, and debate with the best of them, but that's not what he relied on. He had weapons that were not of this world. He had revealed truth, prayer, the Spirit of God, and other forms of divine assistance.

These weapons were capable of "demolishing strongholds" (v. 4). He alluded to them earlier in his letter (6.7, "with weapons of righteousness in the right hand and in the left") and gave his fullest exposition of them in Ephesians 6.10ff. But we shouldn't make the mistake of getting caught up trying to identify the exact weaponry he is referring to here. The bigger point to see is that they are weapons of mass destruction. They brought no harm to humans but absolutely obliterated the sinful facades and structures fabricated by man and utilized by demonic powers (1 Corinthians 10.18–22).

When Paul arrived in Corinth—a city not far removed from Athens and its rich philosophical tradition of Socrates, Plato, and Aristotle, he encountered the speculative wisdom of the world that exalted and magnified man and his understanding. The gospel of Jesus destroyed this and pointed people away from themselves and toward God (see 1 Corinthians 1.18–25, 2.1–5). Was it the idols and the immorality that went with it? The message of Jesus laid waste to its underpinnings and pointed them to the holiness that came through Christ (1 Corinthians 1.1–2, chapters 8–10). Was it the imperial worship of Rome that declared emperors gods upon their death? Paul brought it to nothing by his proclamation of the One who had been resurrected from the dead (1 Corinthians 15.3–7).

In all this, Paul was demolishing "arguments and every pretension that sets itself up against the knowledge of God" and taking "captive every thought" and making it "obedient to Christ" (2 Corinthians 10.5). And it still works today as it brings people out of the darkness of materialism, addiction, worldliness, or whatever false structures they have built their life around. And in its place, God brings about new creation in Christ.

I heard someone recently pushing an outdoor event that was about to take place. This individual wanted a big crowd to be there so a drone could take an overhead shot to give people a view of what things looked like from above. I think that's exactly what disciples need. We need to see things from God's point of view! We're part of tearing down strongholds and structures utilized by the "powers of this dark world and the spiritual forces of evil" (Ephesians 6.12). We're being used by God to build His new creation!

But the alarming fact is that too many of us live uninformed of these truths. Instead of having a view from above, we see things in a flat, one-dimensional way. Too often our status quo is to see ourselves as a nice group of nice people doing nice things. A curse on that! Instead of seeing God at work through us in staggering, cosmic ways, we yawn our way through life. And then we wonder why our churches struggle to keep young people. They want nothing to do with our anesthetized existence! Maybe the better question is how we hang on to anyone at all.

There's nothing compelling about being part of a nice group of nice people doing nice things. There's nothing in it that reaches out to grab us and make us feel that this is something we must be a part of. Instead, we'll be a part of as much or as little as we have the time and inclination to, but if anything we perceive to be bigger comes calling, we won't be there. In short, that's how Jesus Christ loses out to ballgames, weekends at the lake, and a host of other things.

I believe that most people, in their heart of hearts, long to give themselves to something bigger than themselves. They want to experience sacrifice and commitment at deep levels. But they're not going to do this for just anything—it must be something worthy.

We need to bring them face-to-face with the living, breathing Lord of the universe and His call for us to be involved in demolishing strongholds and building new creations with God. We need to help them see that whether it's being a good husband or wife, loving your family, working hard on your job or in school, or whatever we do, we are called to live at a level that touches the eternal and has cosmic significance.

That's the way it looks from God's point of view!

Waking Up Sleepy Saints

"Wake up, sleeper,
rise from the dead,
and Christ will shine on you."
(Ephesians 5.14)

*E*xtra! Extra! Read all about it!

If movies about the past are to be trusted, this is what the newspaper boys on street corners used to shout out (followed by the day's headline) to incite people to buy their papers. Though that day and time is no longer with us, I can't help but think that Paul's little letter to the Ephesians is worthy of this kind of promotion and excitement.

In Ephesians, Paul dares us to stretch our spirits and overflow our hearts with "the unfathomable riches of Christ" (3.8 NASB). He has huge, spectacular truths to share that splash way outside the margins of our minds. He talks to us about being chosen in Christ "before the creation of the world" (1.4). He speaks of God's "eternal purpose" (3.11) and how he wants us to know the love of Christ "that surpasses knowledge" (3.19). This kind of speech is normative to the letter! And yet, many people yawn and wonder what all the fuss is about while tracking the latest movement of their favorite celebrity on social media.

Seriously?

The God of Ephesians is a HUGE God. What am I saying? I'm not suggesting that God isn't presented this way in other parts of the biblical witness, but rather that in Ephesians, this truth is marvelously compressed in the six chapters that form the letter. It's a small sponge that is super absorbent, so every time you squeeze it, it supplies endless amounts of wonder. Paul connects some theological dots in Ephesians that leave in shambles the little boxes in which we place God. He is so much bigger than we can imagine; His purposes are so much grander.

The dimension of time Paul wants to explore is eternity. The concepts he wants to advocate are those that surpass knowledge. The realms he wants to work in are the heavenly realms. The goal he's pointing us toward is the time when God brings "unity to all things in heaven and on earth under Christ" (1.10).

Ephesians will not allow us to think of ourselves as insignificant or our lives as ho-hum. As part of the body of Christ, we bear witness not just on earth but on a cosmic scale (3.10–11). As the body of Christ, God continues the reconciliation and resurrection work through us that He began with Jesus (1.19–21). As soldiers of Christ, we are involved in a daily war "against the rulers, against the authorities, against the powers of this dark world and against the spiritual forces of evil in the heavenly realms" (6.12).

Whatever it might be, Ephesians is a wake-up call for sleepy saints! *Extra! Extra! Read all about it!*

Subversive Joy

"But even if I am being poured out like a drink offering on the sacrifice and service coming from your faith, I am glad and rejoice with all of you."
(Philippians 2.17)

What kind of man is it who, knowing He is just hours away from being subjected to one of the cruelest, most painful, and shameful deaths imaginable —speaks of His joy? How could He possibly talk to His disciples about His joy being complete in them (John 15.11)? What are we to make of this? A person unfamiliar with Christ could dismiss it all as the ranting of someone too close to death to be thinking clearly, but those of us who know Him know better.

That all this says something remarkable about Jesus is not surprising for we have to come to expect the unexpected from Him, haven't we? That it says something about joy is less familiar territory. What it suggests is that joy has a subversive quality to it. Not only is it not what many think it is, it undermines and overthrows much of our thinking about human fulfillment.

The place to begin is by noting that joy is subversive to happiness. It may be that you equate joy and happiness, but I think distinguishing between the two is quite helpful because the concepts behind the words are radically different. If you look up the etymology of the word happiness, you find that it goes back to the word *hap* and is from the same word family as *happenings*. In short, happiness is what occurs when the happenings of life go our way.

Happiness tends to be superficial—we're pleased when the sun is shining, the traffic isn't bad on the way to work, and the weekend is near. It is obviously quite transient in nature—there are rainy days when the traffic is terrible and weekends that we have to work! In fact, the whole happiness approach to life is very much a roller coaster ride. That's why the word originally carried the meaning of *lucky*, and even today, *good fortune* is still given as one of its meanings.

It is amazing how many people believe that Jesus came to make us happy. The prosperity gospel advocates have done a good job catering to our lower/consumer nature and convinced many that life in Christ is *supposed to be* an unending stream of sugar and syrup. When someone experiences something less than that—a sense of entitlement flares up, and prayers are offered like this one posted on a social network in response to a minor injury someone had suffered; "So sorry! We'll pray for speedy healing and no pain." Compare that with what Paul says in Philippians 1.29, "For it has been granted to you on behalf of Christ not only to believe in Him, but also to suffer for Him." I'm not suggesting that every time we hurt it's in God's plans, but I am saying there's something seriously skewed with prayers that leave no room for God's will and treat suffering like Christians have been promised immunity from it.

The good news is that there is something much better than happiness and its corresponding Peter Pan approach to discipleship. It is joy. While the NIV only mentions "happy" or "happiness" about 25 times, "joy" and "rejoice" are found about 400 times. But we must not think of joy as Happiness 2.0. It is not an upgrade on happiness—it's a whole new operating system! Joy isn't based on the right happenings of life. It isn't superficial. It isn't arbitrary. Joy is rooted in a relationship with Jesus. It is part of the fruit the Spirit produces in the disciple's life (Galatians 5.22).

Joy also subverts our pursuit of it. It defies the consumer approach that says we become followers of Jesus so we can have joy and fulfillment. It doesn't work that way. If joy is our primary goal, then we will never possess it. It's only when we die to self and pursue Jesus that joy enters our lives. You can't grow fruit—you can only grow the plant that produces the fruit. In the same way, only when we lose ourselves in following Jesus can we truly experience joy.

One biblical book with quite a bit to say about joy is Paul's letter to the Philippians. I counted 14 times the words joy, rejoice, or glad were used. In true subversive style, Paul is in prison as he writes about joy to the disciples at Philippi. They were privileged to live in an imperial colony (Acts 16.12). This meant they were citizens of Rome with all the privileges—self-government, the protection of Rome, the right of appeal, and freedom from scourging. All these things could lead to a happy life.

But God had something better in mind. The call of Christ led them to become part of a different kingdom with a superior citizenship (Philippians 3.20). Though Lord Caesar's name could be found everywhere in Philippi, their allegiance was to a greater lord (Romans 10.9–10). And through following Him, they experienced something much better than happiness (Philippians 4.4).

Joy is still subversive. It overthrows happiness, refuses to be pursued, and is the product of renouncing our agendas that Christ might reign. If all that sounds counterintuitive, I think that's the point.

The Gratitude of Holiness (1)

Therefore, since we are receiving a kingdom that cannot be shaken, let us be thankful, and so worship God acceptably with reverence and awe, for our "God is a consuming fire." (Hebrews 12.28–29)

The Hebrew writer was challenging the disciples he was addressing to pursue holiness (12.14). As noted in an earlier piece, holiness is wholeness. It is being responsive to God in every area of our lives. As Jesus talked about, it is loving God with all our heart, soul, mind, and strength (Mark 12.30). This doesn't happen accidentally or incidentally, so they were to "make every effort" toward this end. Understood in this context, these words are not an aside or digression but rather part of a crescendo the writer has been building toward throughout the letter.

To stoke the fire even more, he wants them to come to grips with all they have through Christ (v. 22ff). Unlike Israel, they are part of "a kingdom that cannot be shaken" (v. 28). The appropriate response is to be thankful and to worship God with reverence and awe.

Worshiping God with reverence and awe sounds fitting in light of the truth that He is a consuming fire (v. 29), but thankfulness seems a little, well… pedestrian and ordinary. Many of us tend to see it as occupying more of a supporting role. After all, we're supposed to be thankful, we are, and that's that—right? We're ready to move on to something else—something more spiritual.

Maybe it's worth taking a closer look at gratitude.

The words thank, thanks, thankfulness, gratitude, and grateful are found about 150 times in the biblical witness. That's not a large number when compared to other qualities like love (688), faith (458), peace (249) or joy (242), but numbers don't always tell the whole story, do they? Gratitude is an attitude toward God in response to His goodness toward us. This attitude will manifest itself in certain behaviors, to be sure, but it begins in the heart with the open-eyed acknowledgment of the blessings we have received from our Father. This acknowledgment is the soil for the seeds of gratitude to grow in and its fruit can be unlimited.

It was Abraham Heschel who said, "It is gratefulness which makes the soul great." Gratitude makes the soul great not because it is seeking greatness, but by acknowledging its indebtedness to God, it takes on greatness. After all, God doesn't save us because we're great; He saves us because He's great and the great soul acknowledges this.

Gratitude sees God's goodness, that He is "compassionate and gracious, slow to anger, abounding in love . . . He does not treat us as our sins deserve, or repay us according to our iniquities" (Psalm 103.8,10). It sees not only this but a thousand other ways in which God actively blesses and sustains our lives. Put it all together and gratitude forms the foundation for who we are. We love *because* He first loved us.

> *So then, just as you received Jesus Christ as Lord, continue to live your lives in Him, rooted and built up in Him, strengthened in the faith as you were taught, and overflowing with thankfulness. (Colossians 2.6–7)*

What do you suppose he means by that?

The Gratitude of Holiness (2)

Therefore, since we are receiving a kingdom that cannot be shaken, let us be thankful, and so worship God acceptably with reverence and awe, for our "God is a consuming fire." (Hebrews 12.28–29)

The gratitude the writer asks for in Hebrews 12.28 *is to be expressed* in the form of reverence and awe ("let us be thankful and so worship God with reverence and awe"). The "and so" suggests he's interested in gratitude not just for itself but as a means to the worshipful spirit he wants us to possess. This relationship between thankfulness and worship/praise is expressed frequently in the Psalms (Psalm 95.2, 100—esp. v. 4), and it's why praise is often spoken of as giving thanks (Psalms 7.17, 35.18, etc.).

For the Hebrew writer then, if we're not reverent, we're not grateful. To be overly casual with God is not, as some suppose, a mark of great spirituality—it's indicative of a lack of appreciation for who God is and what He's done for us. A simple test of reverence is to ask ourselves, "Is God living in my world or am I living in His?" The first is the default setting of the world, while the latter is the default setting of the kingdom. This is our Father's world!

Recognizing this is our Father's world is an act of bare faith that opens the eyes of our hearts to see what is unseen. Humanity is no longer something that was swimming in the sea, started swinging in a tree, and now it's me. We are "fearfully and wonderfully made." The universe is not a vast, bleak abyss resulting from enormous amounts of time and chance but something that proclaims God's power and majesty.

We might be tempted to think that the worship the writer speaks of has to do with the kind of activities we do in our church buildings, but this doesn't appear to be the case. Although the chapter ends here, the discussion doesn't. The instructions to love one another (13.1), show hospitality to strangers (v. 2), and remember those in prison (v. 3) are all brought up under the umbrella of worshiping God with reverence and awe.

But he doesn't stop there!

He goes on to speak of honoring our marriage vows (v. 4), keeping ourselves free from the love of money and being content with what we have (v. 5). He goes on to mention other things before adding, "And do not forget to do good and to share with others, for with such sacrifices God is pleased" (v. 16). The mention of sacrifices makes it clear that the discussion of worshiping God is still in view.

All of this should open our eyes to a couple of things. Worship is about revering God rather than performative acts. We would do well to recognize the difference. A child's off-key singing of *Jesus Loves the Little Children* is more pleasing to our Father than a professional concert experience in an assembly more concerned about style than substance.

The other truth is that living with reverence to God is a 24/7 activity. It is not only related to how we treat God, but how we treat others. Understood in this light, it takes worship of God out of the building and into every phase of life.

That is what gratitude looks like.

Living as Part Two People

In his great mercy he has given us new birth into a living hope through the resurrection of Jesus Christ from the dead. (1 Peter 1.3)

Death and resurrection are looked upon by many people from a purely Plan B perspective—a fall back position when Plan A (being alive) is no longer possible. We are quite certain we want no part of them until there is absolutely no other option. There's very little of the "to live is Christ and to die is gain" mindset that Paul expressed in Philippians 1.21.

Still, disciples of Jesus have hope (1 Thessalonians 4.13). And the biblical presentation of hope is not about exchanging a greater state of existence for a lesser one. But we can make the mistake of thinking that God looks at things as we do—that He wants no part of these things for us, and that's where things unravel even more.

From a biblical viewpoint, death and resurrection are not Plan B—they are Part Two. Part Two is what is supposed to follow Part One. Like two sections of a book, they are connected, intertwined even so that life is not without death, and death is certainly not without life. Moreover, Part Two is the place where all the joy, goodness, and wonder that were experienced in Part One are *fully realized*.

When we begin to think and live as Part Two people, we display that marvelous attribute touched on earlier—hope. The Hebrew writer speaks of hope as an anchor of the soul (6.19). Drifting in a boat can be a rather helpless feeling. Our youngest daughter, Laura, and I experienced this on one occasion when the engine in our boat stopped and was completely uninterested in restarting. From that point on, the wind and the current had everything to say about where were going and we had no say. We could have used an anchor! When through faith, we arrive at an understanding of and in our Father's promises, we take possession of hope. We understand that everything belongs to Him, and He works all things together for the good of those who love Him (Romans 8.28–39). The rain is still going to come, the wind is still going to blow, but they are neither fatal to nor final for us.

Our story was written long ago in a careful hand by our loving Father. It is one story in two parts with a steady stream of hope running all the way through it. May we learn to embrace both parts, drink deeply of the hope, and live fearlessly and joyfully for Him who died and lives for us.

Changing the World

Slaves, in reverent fear of God submit yourselves to your masters, not only to those who are good and considerate, but also to those who are harsh.
(1 Peter 2.18)

Submission is a prominent theme in 1 Peter. He speaks of the younger being submissive to the older (5.5), wives to their husbands (3.1, 5), slaves to their masters (2.18), and disciples to civil authorities (2.13). Additionally, there are other places where he uses the word "humble" to urge submissive conduct (3.8, 5.5–6). The central section where he develops much of this is in 2.13–3.18. One of the most challenging parts for us is his instructions for slaves to submit to their masters.

Slavery in NT times was not the slavery of the new world where people were kidnapped, put in chains, and sold. Neither was it the servitude of the Mosaic law, which had a rehabilitative function and took people who were on the margins of society due to financial problems or criminal offenses of a minor nature and moved them back toward the center. There was no need for bankruptcy courts or prisons in Israel because people in these situations were absorbed into functional households where they worked for up to six years and then were released and set up for success (Deuteronomy 15.12–15).

The slavery we come across in the New Testament was somewhere between these two extremes. People most often became slaves through birth (if your parents were slaves, then so were you). Large numbers became slaves after they were taken prisoner in war. But it also wasn't uncommon for people to voluntarily enter into slavery for the security and/or upward mobility it could provide. The number of people who were slaves was staggering—depending on who you read, it was anywhere between one-third to two-thirds of the population.

Texts like these can be treated in such a way that the end result is we spend all our time either putting God on trial or defending Him. While there's certainly a time and place for questions along these lines, we need to understand they miss the point of the text. God knew the conditions these disciples were living under better than we ever will, and He told them to submit to their masters and to their everlasting credit and His glory—that's just what they did! We get lost in questioning the command, they got lost in obeying it. Which group sounds like they were living out their freedom (1 Peter 2.16) and proclaiming Jesus (v. 9)? Which group was living out the story of Jesus before the watching world?

We moderns tend to have a bias toward "changing the system." So many of us are convinced we are just one candidate away from changing the world (and we know who that candidate is!). Lots of time and energy is spent advocating, debating, and berating. Yet even when our person gets in, it's not what we hoped for. In this, we are no different than the people who wanted to make Jesus a political king (see John 6.14–15). I suppose politics will always be a hot topic, but it's not the way to change the world. Tolstoy said it best, "Everyone thinks of changing the world, no one thinks of changing himself." Peter agreed with that; the early disciples lived submitted lives, and today Rome is no longer an empire but a tourist destination while the kingdom of Jesus is all over the world.

How do you suppose that happened?

Now, can we get back to a *really important* issue, like why the writers of the biblical witness didn't condemn slavery?

> *Though you have not seen him, you love him; and even though you do not see him now, you believe in him and are filled with an inexpressible and glorious joy.*
> (1 Peter 1.8)

Living with Longing

Each of the four living creatures had six wings and was covered with eyes all around, even under its wings. Day and night they never stop saying. "Holy, holy, holy is the Lord God Almighty, who was, and is, and is to come."
(Revelation 4.8)

No matter where we might find ourselves in the Scripture or life, it seems as if we're never far from the holiness of God. The word "holy" occurs over 500 times in the Bible. Part of the model prayer is "Holy is Your name" (i.e., *Holy are You*). We've touched upon God's holiness in some previous pieces, but to no one's surprise, it's a profoundly rich subject. I want to say just a bit more here and expand on some previous things without repeating myself (too much).

The place to start is by confessing our limitations on this matter. Our ability to understand God's holiness is something like a child's ability to grasp a parent's job. Even if they have a reasonably accurate idea of what that involves, there will still be a huge gap between perception and reality due to the substantial amount of depth and detail absent from their understanding. And why wouldn't there be? Children lack the experiential framework to appreciate everything that is involved in whatever it is their parent does. In the same way, while we can know what God has revealed to us about Himself (Deuteronomy 29.29)—and that is significant, it's also healthy to realize our limitations.

Continuing along the line of our limitations, while we are finite in our nature, God's holiness means He is transcendent. He knows no limits; He has no beginning or end. He is the Uncaused Cause of everything. He possesses the power to *speak* into existence a universe with more stars in it than all the sand on Earth's beaches, deserts, and ocean floors—a universe that defies measurement, denies all attempts to explain it apart from Him, and displays His handiwork everywhere you look. Yes, God did that.

But holiness embraces more than His nature; it also has to do with His perfect character. In contrast to our brokenness and fragmentation, God is whole and complete. He is radically different from us. He is everything we aren't. We are sinful, and He is sinless. He is the epitome of love, truth, justice, mercy, kindness, goodness, and everything else. The Father of everyone is unlike anyone.

Up to this point, most of us are okay. Even if we can't get our minds totally around these concepts—we get the gist of them. God is a universe (or two) beyond us in terms of His nature and character. However, the next point about God's holiness is the most challenging because it takes us in a different direction. This truth isn't hard to grasp because it entails something so far beyond us; we struggle with it because we do understand it.

What is it? It is the fact that God's holiness means that He is, in *some sense*, unapproachable to us. Disciples tend to blanch at this and point out how through Jesus our High Priest, we have access to the very presence of God (Hebrews 10.19ff). And what a glorious truth that is! And yet, the same writer tells us "Our God is a consuming fire" (12.29). Paul tells Timothy that God dwells in unapproachable light "whom no one has seen or can see" (1 Timothy 6.16). Just as looking at the sun would bring blindness, seeing God in His essence would bring death ("No one may see Me and live" — Exodus 33.20). As I said, all of this leaves us somewhat disappointed, slightly uncomfortable, and possibly a bit empty.

Which is probably the way it's supposed to be.

After all, God's not finished with us yet. While it's true the cross work of Jesus has brought us into an intimate relationship with our Father, we have not yet reached the ultimate stage of our relationship with Him. That won't happen in this life, with our body in its present state. The same Jesus who has brought us to the Father will transform our body to be like His glorious body (Philippians 3.20–21). We will see Jesus as He is (1 John 3.1–3) and we will see God (Matthew 5.8).

Until then, we embrace the uncomfortable. We live with a holy longing to see our Father. This is not a bad thing because it roots us in reverence and reminds us that this world is not our home.

Finally, there's this to say: while the holiness of God transcends our ability to understand it, what is unknown by us should not be viewed with anxiety. After all, it is His holy love that has led Him to seek us, save us, and prepare us to be with Him eternally. Jim McGuiggan observes that the One "who takes sin more seriously than we sinners can imagine … never wearies running alongside repentant sinners to offer them forgiveness and help to overcome sin."

What we learned earlier from Isaiah is true in Revelation. And it is still gloriously true today—His holiness is our hope!

> *"I live in a high and holy place, but also with the one who is contrite and lowly in spirit, to revive the spirit of the lowly and to revive the heart of the contrite."* (Isaiah 57.15)

Examples Today

How Deep the Father's Love for Us

For if, while we were God's enemies, we were reconciled to Him through the death of his Son, how much more, having been reconciled, shall we be saved through His life! (Romans 5.10)

I heard the following story on Moth Radio on Father's Day weekend years ago. It's about a husband and wife who had just experienced the birth of their first child—a girl.

The father was sent from the hospital to a grocery store across the street to get a few items. He was on one of the aisles scoping things out when over the store's sound system, the extended version of Stevie Wonder's *Isn't She Lovely* began to play. As you might recall, the song is about the birth of Wonder's daughter (complete with her crying at the beginning).

For our first-time father, it became the tipping point as the magnitude of what had transpired sank in. He and his wife were parents of a beautiful baby girl. Together, they had brought this tiny, precious life into the world. She was now theirs to nurture and raise. Every parent has experienced this moment when the potent combination of blessing and responsibility staggers you, and right there in the middle of aisle 7, he had his. It resulted in what can only be described as a mild meltdown as he dropped to his knees, tears rolling down his cheeks.

However, the tiny part of his still-functioning brain heard the song interrupted by an announcement requesting immediate assistance on aisle 7. He had just enough presence of mind to look up and see that not only was he on aisle 7—he was the only person on the aisle. At just that moment, a teenage bag boy came around the corner and asked him in a squeaky voice if everything was okay. He told him it was and noticed that the young man looked as relieved as he was.

He realized he needed to compose himself and was starting to do so when he saw a man with the word "Manager" on his name badge and he looked angry. He thundered out, "Sir, can I be of assistance to you?" Our father decided to come clean and told him that he came from the hospital across the street where he and his wife just had their first child, a girl. He told him that when the song started playing, he just kind of lost it. At the mention of the song, the store manager stopped and cocked his head to listen because he heard music all day and paid no attention to it.

The next thing our father knew, he was "buried in man" as the arms of the manager went around him. Was he going to call for store security? In the years to come, would his daughter ask him to tell her again the story of how he was arrested on the day she was born?

Then he heard the manager say, "My wife and I just had our first child, a little girl, born two months ago."

And there you have it—just two first-time dads hugging it out in celebration of the joy of fatherhood on aisle 7 of your local grocery store.

For those of us who belong to Christ, it's something more because it's hard to think about how much we love our children without thinking about how much our Father loves us. It was so great that He was willing to give up His firstborn for us.

How deep the Father's love for us—how vast beyond all measure!

I've Never Seen That Before!

Do not be overcome by evil,
but overcome evil with good. (Romans 12.21)

I hope it hasn't been too long since you said or thought these words. Part of what it means to be a disciple of Jesus is to live with our eyes wide open. Life isn't boring. We don't need to be dependent upon others to entertain us. There is wonder all around us if we are open to seeing it.

One of the wonders of life is how God calls us to do things we would probably never dream of doing if it were left up to us. Things like loving our enemies, praying for them, and refusing to repay evil for evil but pursuing peace instead. Jesus speaks to this in Matthew 5.43–48, and Paul does the same in Romans 12.17–21. It's heady, visionary teaching that is not for the faint of heart. More to the point, both Jesus and Paul lived it out, so they didn't just talk about this as if it would be a courageous thing to aspire to—they lived it out under some of the most difficult circumstances imaginable.

When the Gulf War started in 1990, we lived in Sumter, South Carolina. Shaw Air Force Base is located there. We had several military families in the congregation and a few who were in the reserves. One Sunday morning, our time together was devoted to praying for the men and women who were part of Operation Desert Storm. I'll never forget one of the men got up and prayed specifically for Saddam Hussein. If you don't know or remember, he was the leader of Iraq—the country the coalition forces were fighting against. This brother prayed that Saddam Hussein would come to faith in Jesus and experience God's forgiveness. I couldn't remember ever hearing anyone pray anything like that before. (Certainly not me.) And sadly, I can count on one hand, maybe two, the times I've heard anyone do it since then. If we are serious about our prayers being shaped by Scripture, this is something that we should be doing!

A few years ago, a man stood up in a federal courtroom to read a letter. It was addressed to the defendant who was being sentenced to twenty years in prison for selling the drugs that led to the death of the man's twenty-year-old daughter. The letter talked about his daughter's choice to get involved with drugs and how it ended up costing her life. It also talked about the defendant's decision to sell his daughter the drugs with no concern for her life. Then it said this.

By God's love and grace we are saved and forgiven. Forgiveness does not right a wrong, but it frees us from the bondage of that wrong. It also does not free you from the consequences of sin here on earth, but it allows you to be right with God … You need to know that we do not hold any ill feelings toward you as a person created by God. We extend forgiveness to you for the wrongs against our family in the same way that Christ has forgiven our wrongs … We neither hate nor condemn you in any way but hope that through your conviction, you will seek your own personal forgiveness from God.

One of the U.S. attorneys prosecuting the case said he had never seen anything like that before. My guess is that he spoke for most people in that courtroom.

Wouldn't it be great if God's people lived in such a way so that when others saw and experienced such acts of love, mercy and forgiveness we *wouldn't* hear them or anyone else say, "I've never seen that before?"

The Music of Heaven

After Jesus said this, he looked toward heaven and prayed. (John 17.1)

Beatrice Harrison was an accomplished British cellist of the last century whose peak performing years were in the period between the two world wars. One summer evening in 1924, she was practicing in her garden when she stopped and restarted several times. The reason? There was a nightingale that began singing along with her—echoing parts of what she had just played. Beatrice paused to take in its response.

She returned the following evening, and the same thing happened and the night after that as well. After a while, she decided that more people needed to hear this, so she reached out to a fledging organization known as the BBC. They weren't completely sold on her proposal initially, but eventually, she was able to persuade them to do a radio broadcast from her garden.

The engineers came out and did a test run and everything went well. The broadcast was set up for the next evening. They interrupted their regular programming, but for quite some time . . . Beatrice played, but there was no nightingale joining her. Perhaps the production crew had scared it. Finally, with about fifteen minutes left in the broadcast, the nightingale began to sing. The response to the broadcast was overwhelming! They repeated it the following month and every spring after that for the next dozen years. Harrison received some 50,000 letters during this time.

It's a fine thing to think about humans and animals interacting in this way. It suggests an overarching harmony among God's creation that is in keeping with the early chapters of Genesis when Adam named the animals and Noah later gathered them into the ark. These things happened before "the fear and dread" of man came upon wildlife (Genesis 9.2). Maybe when the curse is lifted from creation, as Paul speaks about in Romans 8, man and animals will revert to what we read about there. If so, the scene that played out with Beatrice Harrison and the nightingale is a foretaste of what is to come.

All this made me think about Jesus praying to God in John 17. It's a prayer of enormous depth and beauty. Jesus prays about His Father being glorified (v. 1), the work He's completed in revealing God to the disciples (v. 4, 6–8), for His disciples to be protected from the evil one, sanctified in the truth and sent into the world (v. 15–18), the unity of future believers (v. 20–21), and even our final destiny with Him in heaven (v. 24). What is there to say about such a prayer? Only this. when Jesus prayed, heaven must have sung in response.

Many of us (myself included) have a long way to go in our prayer lives—and we recognize it! But we're pleased beyond words that we see in Jesus both what God desires us to be and what we want to be. We're so proud of Him and the heroic choices He made at every turn in His life. Philippians 2.5–11 says that's why God made Him Lord. We gladly serve Him as our sovereign because He is what we rejoice in and want to be ourselves.

He is the music of heaven!

Food on our Plate and Music in the Metro

"When you received the word of God, which you heard from us, you accepted it not as a human word, but as it actually is, the word of God, which is indeed at work in you who believe." (1 Thessalonians 2.13)

I doubt if it takes too much work for most of us to recall those times as a child when we didn't feel like eating what was on our plates. It's close to a rite of passage. A common strategy employed by many of us on such occasions was to push the food around to make it look as if we'd actually eaten something. A counter-strategy employed by our parents (after they had told us about hungry children in other parts of the world) was to remind us that food on the plate couldn't provide the nourishment we needed as long as it remained there. I remember my father would say, "I want to see that food on the inside looking out."

I wonder if sometimes, in our exploration of God's word, we don't fall into the same kind of thing and end up pushing a few verses around on our plate rather than internalizing them and allowing them to nurture us. We look at the text before us and mentally recite familiar factoids instead of seeking the answer to penetrating questions like. What is the big truth being communicated here? What would this have meant to the original audience? How does it speak to our lives today? What is God saying to me through this text? In what ways will this help me walk more closely with Him? If we haven't addressed important questions like these, we're missing out on important spiritual nutrients.

All of this is predicated on our understanding that the biblical witness is not a collection of dry, dead documents—it is "living and active" (Hebrews 4.12). It is a message between a Father and His children. Paul told the church at Thessalonica he was grateful for them because they received his message "not as a human word, but as it actually is, the word of God, which is indeed at work in you who believe" (1 Thessalonians 2.13). Dead churches have a dead word, lukewarm churches have a lukewarm word, but living churches have a living word! Armed with this conviction, time in the word becomes biblical exploration with treasures to be unearthed at every turn.

The scene at the Washington D.C. metro was a familiar one—people were heading to work on a Friday morning in January. The location of this particular station meant that most of them were employed by the federal government. Near one of the entrances, a thirty-nine-year-old man stood by a trashcan playing a violin. He wore jeans, a tee shirt, and a baseball cap. The violin case was open and there were a few bills and coins in it. He would play for about 45 minutes as almost 1,100 people passed by. Only 7 people stopped to listen before moving on; 27 dropped in some money (totaling a little over 32 dollars), and 1,070 people went by without pausing.

The man was Joshua Bell—a world-class violinist. Three days before he had performed in front of a full house at Symphony Hall in Boston. The violin he was playing was a Stradivarius valued at 3.5 million dollars. He was part of an experiment conducted by the Washington Post to see if commuters would notice the presence of the extraordinary among them. They didn't. If they saw anything at all, it was a street musician playing music and trying to make a few bucks.

What they missed was a free performance of some of the greatest music known to man—Bach, Schubert, Mendelssohn, etc. The shoeshine lady complained that he was too loud. The people standing in line to buy lottery tickets, hoping to one day get lucky, were clueless about the remarkably good fortune just a few feet away from them.

This is exactly the way it is with Scripture. We can look at it from a single level—the "I'm just passing through quickly on my way somewhere" perspective. We won't see much—surface things that are often as confusing as clarifying. Or we can take time to explore its many layers and be enriched, challenged, blessed, and shaped by God's words for us.

I recently heard about a single mother raising two teenage sons. Their drive to school takes thirty minutes and they spend that time listening to the word of God. Isn't that interesting (and maybe a little convicting)? Here is a busy person with a lot on her plate (she teaches school and has somehow also managed to recently earn a PhD), but she makes it a priority for herself and her family to hear what God has to say.

What do you think makes people do things like that?

> *The precepts of the Lord are right, giving joy to the heart.*
> *The commands of the Lord are radiant, giving light to the eyes.*
> (Psalm 19.8)

A Great Place to Be

Rejoice always, pray continually, give thanks in all circumstances; for this is God's will for you in Christ Jesus. (1 Thessalonians 5.16–18)

Beverly Gaventa notes how "prayerful thanksgiving dominates 1 Thessalonians." Paul pauses three times in the first three chapters to give thanks (1.2, 2.13, 3.9). At the end of the letter, he encourages the disciples to "give thanks in all circumstances" (5.18). In all of this, he's not simply repeating himself nor is he trying to meet some quota—his life is overflowing with gratitude and he has to say something about it! He's also modeling the way we are meant to live.

Scott Macaulay lives in Melrose, Massachusetts, where he runs *Macaulay's House of Vacuum Cleaners*. But that's not what he's known for—Scott is known for Thanksgiving.

It started in 1985, when Scott was 24. His parents were getting divorced, and to make matters worse, there was nothing amicable about it. No one was talking to anyone. With Thanksgiving approaching, he didn't feel like he could spend it with either parent without alienating the other. But Scott hated the thought of eating alone.

He came up with the idea of inviting a dozen strangers to come eat with him. He placed an ad in the paper to that effect and twelve people showed up to share a Thanksgiving meal with Scott. He enjoyed it so much he has been doing it every year since then.

The numbers have swelled as he now feeds anywhere from 60 to 100 people, but the concept remains the same. Having outgrown his house, they meet in the fellowship room of Scott's church. He brings in couches, recliners, rugs, and fake fireplaces to create an "at home" feel. A couple of rooms are set up where appetizers are served, and people can visit before dinner.

As you might imagine, there are some stories.

One year, a woman with Parkinson's came. She hadn't been outside the nursing home she was in for seven years and paid an ambulance $200 to bring her. She was decked out for the occasion and had such a wonderful time that she cried when it was time to leave. One year, a man came who had recently lost his wife. When dinner was over, he put her apron on and helped Scott do the dishes. Then, there was the woman who showed up for leftovers because she lived in a car and was too embarrassed by her situation to come in for the meal. She was so touched by the occasion that she sang a moving rendition of *Amazing Grace*. Finally, there was the year both of Scott's parents showed up. His mother was dying of cancer and wanted them all to be together. She sat on the couch with Scott's father, and the two of them held hands like they were an old married couple.

If you show up for Thanksgiving in Melrose, the one thing you will always be asked to do is to take the time to write on a scrap of paper what you are thankful for. Scott said, "That changes the outlook, from whatever reason they're coming to the dinner to a positive outlook because you start concentrating on what you're thankful for."

He's right. Giving thanks is like flipping a switch. We leave behind the world dialed in on acquisitions to step into a universe that is bright with innumerable stars twinkling with the known and unknown we have to be thankful for. To live here, rather than just making occasional visits, is one of the most radical acts we will ever participate in. The psalmist spoke about entering the temple with thanksgiving and praise in our hearts (Psalm 100.4). Living with a grateful heart takes us through the gate and into the courts of God.

And that's a great place to be!

A Little Debbie Christmas

"It is more blessed to give than to receive" (Acts 20.35).

Two days before Christmas in 2020, one of our friends was down with Covid. She was a schoolteacher and she and her husband had a little girl. Of course, she had to remain isolated from both of them—at Christmas! It was a real bummer, to say the least, but it was just one of those new realities we were all going through, and there wasn't anything anyone could do about it.

Or maybe there was.

I talked to her husband to get an update on her and how they were making it. I asked if we could do anything, and he said, "Not unless you know where I could get some little Debbie Christmas Cakes. She really likes those, and I can't find them anywhere."

Even though Little Debbie and her band of tempting treats hadn't been on my radar in years, I thought I would give it a try. I asked him where he had looked and he mentioned the usual suspects. Then I thought of a place he hadn't mentioned. If you could find them anywhere, they would be there.

I stopped at this store, went in, and went to where the Little Debbie items were displayed. And it just so happened that two distributors were re-stocking the shelves! I told them what I was looking for and they laughed and said something to the effect of, "Yeah, you and everyone else." I figured I had nothing to lose, so I told them the story of the Covid-stricken, school-teaching young mother and one of them looked at me and said, "C'mon, let's go out and see if we have anything in the truck."

As we walked toward the truck, he told me he didn't know if there would be anything in there or not. They were such a hot item that they got rid of them as soon as they got them. I told him I understood and thanked him for taking the time to check it out. I appreciated how busy they were this time of year and the favor he was doing me.

When we got to the truck, he handed me a plastic bag and said, "Hold this open." Now, the back of their delivery truck looked about as cluttered as the bed of my pickup truck, so he had to rummage around a bit. But before too long, he produced a box of—Little Debbie Christmas Cakes! He plopped it in the bag. I was ecstatic! "Thank you so much! I think this is really going to lift her spirits," I said. "Hold on," he said, "Let's see if we have any more." He did.

Another box was dropped into the bag. And then another, and another. When he was done, I had five boxes of Little Debbie Christmas Cakes for our friend. I had started out thinking if I could find just one it would be nothing short of a spectacular success and now, I had five. I was overwhelmed. I tried to pay the man, but he wouldn't take anything, so I thanked him repeatedly.

My friend met us outside his house. We had brought a meal for them. I told him I didn't get a box of Little Debbie Christmas Cakes. He was understanding and said he hadn't expected me to find any.

Then I told him I got five boxes, and he looked at me like I was crazy.

I produced the bag and told him the story.

I never got the name of the man who gave me the five boxes of Little Debbie Christmas Cakes. I should have, but I was too carried away by the moment. But I know this, as long as I'm alive, I'll be telling the story of the Little Debbie Christmas man and how he absolutely made our friend's day by what he did.

For as Jesus came into this world to teach and show us, *"It is more blessed to give than to receive"* (Acts 20.5).

Afterword

A few years before her death, Queen Elizabeth and Richard Griffin, the man who served as her protection officer for 14 years, were hiking in the highlands not far from her castle in Balmoral. They came across two tourists from America who were on a "walking holiday." The Queen always made it a point to stop and talk to fellow hikers, so she greeted the pair and as they engaged in conversation it was clear they didn't recognize her. To be fair, her appearance wasn't what most people were used to seeing as she was dressed down in clothes suitable for hiking.

As they talked, one of the hikers asked if she lived in the area. She explained that she lived in London but had a "house just over the hills." They wanted to know how long she had been coming up there and she told them over eighty years—since she was a little girl. Then came the clincher. Had she ever met the Queen who had a place up here somewhere?

The Queen told them she hadn't but then pointed to Griffin and said that he met with her regularly. They asked Griffin what she was like and he told them, "She can be quite cantankerous at times, but she's got a lovely sense of humor." The tourists *oohed* and *aahed* at this and before you knew it, one of them had placed a camera in the Queen's hand so that she could take a picture of him with Griffin. She graciously obliged.

After the picture was taken, Griffin took the camera from the Queen and quickly took a picture of her with the tourists. Then off they went—neither aware of anything other than they had their picture made with a man who knew the Queen—and the woman who was with him.

This is why history is so much better than fantasy. You can make up fantasy, but you can't make up history—even when it sounds like fantasy.

I love this story because of the insider humor between the Queen and Richard Griffin. She displayed absolutely no hesitancy in throwing him under the bus when the hikers asked if she had ever met the Queen. And he gave it right back to her when they asked him what the Queen was like. It sounds like they had a great friendship and having that is a blessing from God.

And then when one of them put the camera in the Queen's hands and asked her to take a picture of them with Richard Griffin, it's funny, but it's also poignant **because he was satisfied with much less than what the moment was made for them to have.** He could have a picture with the Queen, but all he wanted was a picture with Griffin instead. Sigh.

How often does this happen to us? We are satisfied with less than what we were made for. Our Heavenly Father created us in His image—He made nothing else in that way. He did that because He wants us to share in His life. He wants to bless us. He wants us to have dominion over the world He created.

But so many people are satisfied to live with so much less. It makes me think of Jesus standing outside Jerusalem on His final visit to the city. As He looked upon the city, He wept—not for Himself and the crucifixion He was about to suffer, but because of what He wanted for them and their unwillingness to accept it!

This happened with the tourists because **they gave royalty a quick look over and decided she wasn't.** They didn't mean anything by it, but nonetheless, that's what they did. And people are doing the same thing with Christ today, aren't they? They don't decide that Jesus isn't royalty after carefully reading through the gospels—they make it based on a bad experience someone they know had with some group they heard about. They make their decision because of a celebrity's rant or because none of their friends follow Jesus. They put more thought into what their coffee order will be than they do about the One who loves them more than they love themselves!

But here's where our story turns because Richard Griffin, on his own, took a picture of them with the Queen. **He made provision for them despite their rejection of royalty.** He realized that sooner or later they would look back on their encounter and realize they had been with the Queen. They would have a picture of themselves with the Queen's protection officer—but not one with the Queen! They would spend the rest of their lives ruing the opportunity they let slip through their fingers.

What Griffin did was an act of grace. He made provision for their negligence. Now they would be able to look back and laugh at their folly because they had a picture of themselves with the Queen—how great was that?

In the same way, Romans 5.6–8 tells us that God has made provision for us through Jesus Christ. "While we were still sinners"—hiking through this world with no thought of God—He did for us through Jesus what we couldn't do for ourselves. The cross occurred so that we might have glorious life through Him. How great is that? We'll never look back and laugh at our sins, but we'll rejoice in God's provision despite them.

There's more. Like Griffin, **Jesus is our protection officer.** John says this in 1 John 2.1–2.

My dear children, I write this to you so that you will not sin. But if anybody does sin, we have an advocate with the Father—Jesus Christ, the Righteous One. He is the atoning sacrifice for our sins, and not only for ours but also for the sins of the whole world.

The truth is, **everyone on this planet is searching for something** (whether they are aware of it or not). The answer isn't found in material things—you can have everything to live with, but if you don't have something to live for, you will be empty. It's not fame—look what the famous people do—they can't go anywhere and end up living in seclusion. It's not found in accumulating experiences, traveling the world, or anything other than a relationship with God through Jesus.

What everyone is looking for is God (whether they know it or not). He has set eternity in our hearts (Ecclesiastes 3.11). Augustine said we were made for God, and we are restless until we find Him.

He's not that hard to find. That's what Paul told the Athenians when he said, "From one man he made all the nations, that they should inhabit the whole earth; and he marked out their appointed times in history and the boundaries of their lands. God did this so that they would seek him and perhaps reach out for him and find him, though he is not far from any one of us" (Acts 17.26–27). And how could He be? He provides us with our daily bread (Matthew 6.11), He "fills your hearts with joy" (Acts 14.17), and "in Him we live move and have our being" (Acts 17.28).

Someone said there are two important days in your life—the day you were born and the day you find out why you were born. If you didn't know about God's purpose for you through Jesus, then today has become that day because you were born to be in relationship with God.

If this is that day, read Acts 2 and do what 3,000 others did to find new life in Christ.

Selected Bibliography

Brueggemann, Walter, *Genesis*, Westminster John Knox Press, 1982.

Cheney, Lois A., *God Is No Fool*, Abingdon Press, 1969.

Dyck, Drew, *Yawning at Tigers*, Nelson Books, 2014.

Gladwell, Malcom, *The Tipping Point*, Little Brown, 2000.

Gordon, Arthur, *A Touch of Wonder*, Guidepost Associates, Inc., 1974.

Heschel, Abraham, *I Asked for Wonder*, (Samuel H. Dresner, editor), The Crossroad Publishing Company, 1988.

Lehner, Ulrich L., *God Is Not Nice*, Ava Maris Press, 2017.

Marchant, James (compiler), *Anthology of Jesus*, (Warren Wiersbe, editor), Kregel Publications, 1981.

Mays, James Luther, Psalms. Interpretation. *A Bible Commentary for Preaching and Teaching*, John Know Press, 1994.

McCollough, Donald, *The Trivialization of God*, NavPress, 1995.

McGuiggan, Jim, *Celebrating the Wrath of God*, WaterBrook Press, 2001.

McGuiggan, Jim, *Spending Time with Jim McGuiggan*, Jim McGuiggan. Wordpress.com, 2016.

Sproul, R. C., *The Holiness of God*, Ligonier Ministries, 2010.

www.ingramcontent.com/pod-product-compliance
Lightning Source LLC
Chambersburg PA
CBHW041925090426
42743CB00020B/3439